History of the Housing Crisis

POLEMICS

Polemics draws on radical political philosophy and theory to address directly the various crises that have plagued global society and capitalism in the past decade. The series presents radical critiques of and alternative visions to the existing way of doing things. The texts in this series represent philosophically rigorous but polemical interventions in contemporary global, financial, political, environmental and theoretical crises.

The series is published in partnership with CAPPE, University of Brighton.

Series Editors: Mark Devenney and Clare Woodford

Kidnapped Democracy
Ramón A. Feenstra

Against Free Speech
Anthony Leaker

History of the Housing Crisis
Rebecca Searle

History of the Housing Crisis

Rebecca Searle

ROWMAN & LITTLEFIELD
Lanham • Boulder • New York • London

Published by Rowman & Littlefield
An imprint of The Rowman & Littlefield Publishing Group, Inc.
4501 Forbes Boulevard, Suite 200, Lanham, Maryland 20706
www.rowman.com

86-90 Paul Street, London EC2A 4NE

British Library Cataloguing in Publication Information Available

Library of Congress Cataloging-in-Publication Data

Names: Searle, Rebecca, author.
  Title: History of the housing crisis / Rebecca Searle.
  Description: Lanham : Rowman & Littlefield, [2023] | Series: Polemics |
    Includes bibliographical references and index.
  Identifiers: LCCN 2022037666 (print) | LCCN 2022037667 (ebook) | ISBN
    9781786616241 (cloth) | ISBN 9781786616258 (paperback)
    | ISBN 9781786616265 (ebook)
  Subjects: LCSH: Public housing--Great Britain--History. | Housing--Great
    Britain--History.
  Classification: LCC HD7288.78.G3 S45 2023 (print) | LCC HD7288.78.G3
    (ebook) | DDC 363.5/80941--dc23/eng/20220830
  LC record available at https://lccn.loc.gov/2022037666
  LC ebook record available at https://lccn.loc.gov/2022037667

Contents

For Raya Carmi, who loved to learn
1942–2022

Introduction

The right to adequate housing was first recognized in international law by the 1948 Universal Declaration of Human Rights, yet more than seventy years later there are estimated to be 1.8 billion people globally who do not have access to this basic necessity.[1] Seeking to understand why we are so far from realizing this right in practice, Raquel Rolnik, the former UN Special Rapporteur for Housing, points to "the practical and ideological hegemony of a specific model of housing policy: one based on the promotion of home ownership through market purchase via credit loans."[2] The emergence of this paradigm has been accompanied by a:

> conceptual transformation of adequate housing from a social good into a commodity and a strategy for household wealth accumulation and welfare security. Housing has become a financial asset . . . and housing markets are increasingly regulated so as to promote the financial aspects rather than the social aspects of housing. The real estate sector is perceived as a potential driving force for continued and sustainable economic growth.[3]

As houses become assets rather than homes and policies are enacted that encourage the appreciation of those assets, rising housing costs erode what access populations once had to adequate housing.

The impact of this policy paradigm varies across the world, dependent upon the politics and particular history of each nation. In the UK, Rolnik found "a critical situation in terms of availability, affordability and access to adequate housing."[4] She details how since the 1980s, British housing policy supported an exceptionally high rate of house price growth, enriching the few but making it much harder for those on low and middle incomes to secure adequate housing. With only fragments remaining of a much vaunted public housing system, most have little choice but to live in the private rented sector, where insecure tenancies and the extent of overcrowding and poor housing conditions mean that many tenants are unable to meaningfully realize their

1

right to adequate housing. Rolnik contrasts the contemporary crisis with the achievements of previous policymakers: "Access to adequate housing has been a hallmark of the history of public polices in the United Kingdom. For generations, women and men have progressively given shape to the notion that a dignified life includes access to decent and fair housing regardless of level of income or other status."[5] Supported by policies such as council house building and rental regulation, across the midcentury evermore of the population were able to realise their right to housing. But since the 1980s, successive governments dismantled this infrastructure and focused policy instead on the creation of debt-encumbered owner occupiers, leading to a marked regression in access to housing. It is this regression that is particularly problematic for Rolnik, as the 1966 International Covenant on Economic, Social and Cultural Rights not only reaffirms the right to adequate housing but "the continuous improvement of living conditions." She maintains that "states are bound to provide an equal or better level of enjoyment of a particular right, taking special care to avoid unjustified retrogressive measures."[6] Given the disjuncture between the promise of past policy and the contemporary crisis, Britain has failed to live up to this obligation.

Rolnik describes Britain as one of "the epicentres and laboratories for the development of models of debt financed ownership which have been exported around the world with disastrous consequences."[7] She locates the development of this model in the neoliberal turn of the late 1970s. This book traces the longer history of the crisis and demonstrates the ways in which the policies that were enacted in the 1980s were part of a much longer tradition of British Conservativism. This history enhances not only our understanding of the contemporary housing crisis but also our perspective on the transformations associated with the neoliberal turn.[8]

This book tells three stories that are central to understanding the emergence of the contemporary housing paradigm in Britain. The first explores the ascendency of owner occupation. Over the last century there was a dramatic increase in the proportion of Britons who owned their own homes. While less than a quarter of the population were owner occupiers in 1918, by the end of the century more than 70 percent were.[9] This is often explained away as the fulfilment of a natural desire to own, something Margaret Thatcher claimed was "basic to the spirit of man" and David Cameron thought was "the most natural instinct."[10] There is nothing natural about the desire to own, nor the ideas of property that underpin this notion of ownership. This was an order actively created by the state. Our very idea of property was made by some of the earliest generations of parliamentarians as they sought to wrest power from the monarch. Through practices of expropriation and enclosure at home and abroad, this landholding class developed a new idea of private property that once codified as law was used to justify not only the enclosure of England but the expropriation of a vast global empire. Through these processes emerged the modern British state: a hierarchical property order governed by a parliament of property owners elected by other property owners.

The process of democratisation posed a profound challenge to this order. By the mid-1880s, the propertyless dominated the electorate. Liberals sought to capture the votes of the newly enfranchised by appealing to deeply held popular grievances about the dispossession of the people from the land. Initially this took the form of a pledge to democratise ownership of the land, but by the end of the century far more radical ideas were ascendant that challenged the very idea that absolute property rights pertained to land. In Ireland, the customary rights that tenants held over the land found legal recognition, while in Britain, a land tax introduced in 1909 was based on the premise that landowners had no right to derive profit from the general inflation in land prices. These radical ideas are a source of inspiration today, but the most enduring legacy of this politics was the way it shaped the development of modern Conservativism. To defend the institution of property, Conservatives assimilated more moderate Liberal positions to argue for the redistribution of land through the allocative function of the market, financed through borrowing. They placed faith in the "magic of property," the belief that ownership would perform an educative function and interpellate responsible and virtuous subjects to buttress the existing order against the revolutionary potential of democratisation. Through the promise of a market-led redistribution of property, Conservatives forged a powerful appeal to actual and aspirant owners to defend property from the grips of "socialism."

This antisocialist rhetoric became a key mantra of British Conservativism across the twentieth century as they contended with their new foe: Labour. From the interwar years, Conservatives contrasted their vision of a property-owning democracy with the state-led housing solutions of Labour. They seized upon shortcomings in Labour's housing programmes as a symbol of the broader failure of socialism and pressed the message that only under the Conservatives, and the forces of free market capitalism, would the people acquire the homes they desired. The problem was that the free market could not provide the people with the houses they needed, and across the mid-century, increasing amounts of state subsidies were directed to support the expansion of owner occupation. As the proportion of owner occupiers crept towards 50 percent, Labour worried about the electoral implications of the Conservatives' dichotomous presentation of housing policy and by the 1960s, Labour came out in support of the property-owning democracy. Under this new consensus, ever more public funds were used to support the expansion of home ownership. It is estimated that across the twentieth century, £180 billion was spent propping up owner occupation compared to £396 billion spent on council housing.[11] This is not including the enormous asset transfer initiated under Right to Buy, when between 1980 and 1997 more than 2.2 million council houses worth an estimated £22 billion were sold at massively discounted rates.[12] There is therefore nothing natural about the dominance of owner occupation in contemporary Britain. This was an order actively created by the state at massive cost to the public purse.

The second chapter tells the story of the rise and fall of a very different vision of how to house the people. Rapid urbanization crowded the poor into the most abysmal housing, but it also created the conditions for people to organize and demand better housing. More than any other event, it was the rent strikes of 1915 that shaped the course of British housing policy in the twentieth century. Thanks to the actions of a group of women in Glasgow, the government was forced to introduce rent controls. As much as subsequent Conservative governments tried to remove them, it was not until 1988 that controls were finally lifted. Moreover, by creating a crisis in the private rented sector, at a time when events in Russia and a war-hardened working class made the establishment decidedly nervous, the women of Glasgow played a key role in instituting the bold programme of council house building embarked upon in 1919. Across the mid-twentieth century, governments of both parties contributed to one of the most ambitious state housing programmes, which, at its peak in the early 1980s, accommodated nearly a third of households.[13] Although there were still many who lacked adequate housing, thanks to rent controls and council housing, the British were better housed than they ever had been—or would be.

The Conservatives were never happy with the responsibility the state had assumed to house the people, but for most of the twentieth century were only able to chip away at this with policies that were quickly reversed when Labour was returned to power. In the particular political and economic circumstances of the 1980s, Thatcher's government was able to achieve a more fundamental disavowal of the state's responsibilities towards housing. But what was most significant in the long run was that when Labour was finally returned to power in 1997, it did not contest the Conservative vision; rather, it accepted and extended Conservative policies, overseeing a return to the housing conditions the earliest generations of Labour activists fought so hard against.

Although the majority of Britons today like to think of themselves as homeowners, fewer than 35 percent own their houses outright.[14] The rest are debtors to varying degrees. Collectively, British households owe a staggering £1.23 trillion on their homes.[15] The final chapter therefore tells the story of the growth of the housing finance industry. For much of the twentieth century, the mortgage market in Britain was dominated by building societies. These institutions had their roots in working-class mutual organisations but by the end of the nineteenth century were transformed beyond recognition into powerful financial institutions. Across the mid-twentieth century, building societies provided most of the finance that sustained the rise in owner occupation. As the drive to increase home ownership became ever more politically important, and as this growth became increasingly central to the wider economic health of the nation, the state and the societies were drawn into a symbiotic relationship. Although building societies were keen to promote themselves as models of financial probity, in a competitive market, societies sought to lend to lower-income households by devising mechanisms that displaced the risk of default. These illegal practices threatened not only the collapse of the societies but the stability of the broader economy, leaving the government little choice but to legislate and retrospectively legalise the building societies' activities. By the end of the 1930s, several key features of the contemporary housing finance industry were already evident: the displacement of risk to enable lending to lower-income households, a symbiotic relationship with the state, a national economy dependent on housing finance to fuel growth, and the instability this dependence engenders.

Investment in property, we are told, is as safe as houses, but this is far from the case. The property market experienced a series of booms and busts across the twentieth and early twenty-first centuries. As early as the 1930s, there were signs of a brewing property crash averted only by war.[16] The pattern of boom and bust was repeated in the 1970s and 1980s as rising inflation forced interest rate hikes that hit the bloated property market hard. The entrance of banks into the mortgage market from the 1980s exacerbated these problematic tendencies, opening the floodgates for a tidal wave of debt that fueled spiraling house prices. This was politically convenient, as house price inflation kept owners spending despite wages falling as a proportion of gross domestic product (GDP). A range of financial instruments, such as securitization, enabled lenders to once more distance themselves from the risks associated with lending to low-income households. These risks were instead dissipated across the world economy, so when a subprime mortgage crisis struck the United States in 2007, it triggered a global financial crisis. So economically dependent were nations on the financial institutions that caused this mess, they were deemed "too big to fail" and bailed out at enormous cost to taxpayers.

Rather than learning from this experience, housing finance has been allowed to become more powerful in the post-crisis world. Billions have been spent incentivising lenders to release ever more finance into the economy to defend the wealth already invested in the housing market by an aging, privileged, and increasingly indebted class of homeowners. All the while, policy appears indifferent to the plight of the growing proportion who are unable to realise their right to adequate housing. This book concludes by surveying the state of housing in contemporary Britain, in dialogue with the longer history of crisis, to suggest a range of measures that would help better house the people: tried and tested policies including social housing and rent regulation; the promises of the past that never came to fruition, like land taxation; and the avenues never pursued, such as cooperative housing.

NOTES

1. UN Human Rights, Office of the High Commissioner, "Guidelines for the Implementation of the Right to Adequate Housing," accessed 25 April 2022, https://www.ohchr.org/en/special-procedures/sr-housing/guidelines-implementation-right-adequate-housing.

2. Raquel Rolnik, *Urban Warfare: Housing under the Empire of Finance* (Verso Books, 2019), 4.

3. UN Human Rights, Office of the High Commissioner, "The Impact of Housing Finance Policies on the Right to Adequate Housing of Those Living in Poverty," point 11, accessed 25 April 2022, https://undocs.org/A/67/286.

4. Raquel Rolnik, "Report of the Special Rapporteur on Adequate Housing as a Component of the Right to an Adequate Standard of Living, and on the Right to Non-Discrimination in This Context," 30 December 2013, 7, https://digitallibrary.un.org/record/766907.

5. Rolnik, "Report of the Special Rapporteur," 4.

6. Rolnik, "Report of the Special Rapporteur," 19.

7. Rolnik, *Urban Warfare*, 4.

8. On the problems with the idea of a neoliberal rupture, see Aled Davies, Ben Jackson, and Florence Sutcliffe-Braithwaite, *The Neoliberal Age? Britain since the 1970s* (UCL Press, 2021).

9. Department for Levelling Up, Housing and Communities, and Ministry of Housing, Communities and Local Government, "English Housing Survey Data on Tenure Trends and Cross Tenure Analysis," accessed 25 April 2022, https://www.gov.uk/government/statistical-data-sets/tenure-trends-and-cross-tenure-analysis.

10. Peter Saunders, "Restoring a Nation of Home Owners," Civitas: Institute for the Study of Civil Society, 12 June 2016, 9, http://civitas.org.ukhttps://www.civitas.org.uk/publications/restoring-a-nation-of-home-owners/.

11. In 2000s prices. Alan Holmans, "Historical Statistics of Housing in Britain," Cambridge Centre for Housing and Planning Research, 22 April 2015, 363–65, https://www.cchpr.landecon.cam.ac.uk/Research/Start-Year/2005/Other-Publications/Historical-Statistics-of-Housing-in-Britain.

12. Aled Davies, "'Right to Buy': The Development of a Conservative Housing Policy, 1945–1980," *Contemporary British History* 27, no. 4 (1 December 2013): 421, https://doi.org/10.1080/13619462.2013.824660.

13. Department for Levelling Up, Housing and Communities, and Ministry of Housing, Communities and Local Government, "English Housing Survey Data on Tenure Trends and Cross Tenure Analysis."

14. Ministry of Housing, Communities and Local Government, "English Housing Survey 2020 to 2021: Headline Report," accessed 25 April 2022, https://www.gov.uk /government/statistics/english-housing-survey-2020-to-2021-headline-report.

15. Office for National Statistics, "Household Debt: Wealth in Great Britain," accessed 25 April 2022, https://www.ons.gov.uk/peoplepopulationandcommunity/ personalandhouseholdfinances/incomeandwealth/datasets/householddebtwealthingr eatbritain.

16. George Speight, *Building Society Behaviour and the Mortgage Lending Market in the Interwar Period : Risk-Taking by Mutual Institutions and the Interwar House-Building Boom.* (PhD diss., University of Oxford, 2000).

Chapter 1

Property

THE MAKING OF PROPERTY

In 1788, Mary Houghton, a fifty-eight-year-old resident of the parish of Timworth, Suffolk, was prosecuted for trespass. She had been caught gathering grain left in the fields after harvest, a practice known as gleaning. Gleaning was one of many customary rights the people claimed over the land. The most important were grazing rights, either on cultivated fields after harvest or on common pastures. There were also rights to forage food and to gather fuel and other essential materials from uncultivated land. Rights, and the question of who could exercise those rights, varied from place to place, but collectively this set of customs gave people access to the resources necessary to sustain a way of life and a fragile independence. In her defence, Mary claimed that she was not trespassing because gleaning was a right recognised under common law. The judge had little sympathy and, setting an important legal precedent, ruled that no one could claim a right to glean under common law because it was inconsistent with "the nature of property which imports exclusive enjoyment."[1] Mary was found guilty and fined £35 5s.

This idea of land as exclusive property was in stark contrast to the feudal land order. As land was given in common by God, all land was controlled by the crown. The monarch granted land rights to the nobility in exchange for loyalty, military service, and payment. This gave them the power to dispose of land and collect any fees or rents accruing from it. There were often many layers of rights holders between the person granted the land by the crown and the manorial lords who extracted rents from tenants. None, however, had absolute rights, as the monarch recognised that tenants had a set of customary rights over the land, be that to graze, gather fuel, or glean. So rather than something that was owned exclusively by one person, land in medieval England was governed by a network of rights and obligations. Long before

9

the ruling in the Houghton case, very new ideas about the governance of the land emerged in practice.

In the centuries following the Black Death of 1349–1356, which killed at least a third of the population, there was an increased concentration of land-holding. By agreement, purchase, or force, land was taken out of common use and bounded as private property. The pace of enclosure was particularly rapid in the late fifteenth and early sixteenth centuries as whole villages were cleared to make way for lucrative sheep farming. By 1550, 45 percent of England was enclosed, giving rise to a pattern of agriculture quite different to the rest of Europe.[2] While most European agriculture was dominated by peasants farming little pieces of land, in England there were a smaller number of larger farms, creating competition for leases. Landlords sought to exact more rental income by replacing customary leases, which were let each year for a fixed sum, with economic rents determined by the highest bidder on the market. If they were to survive, tenant farmers had to increase their productivity, and this was usually achieved through the greater use of waged labour, drawing on the ranks of the dispossessed, who, denied access to the land, had no recourse but to sell their labour to purchase necessities. Both farmers and labourers were therefore dependent on the market for access to the most basic means of survival and reproduction. For Ellen Meiksins Wood, it is this form of property relations that was the critical precondition for the emergence of capitalism, for once "market imperatives set the terms of social reproduction, all economic actors . . . are subject to the demands of competition, increasing productivity, capital accumulation, and the intense exploitation of labour."[3] The judge ruling in Mary Houghton's case articulated these logics when he dismissed the right to glean as injurious to the poor:

> Their sustenance can only arise from the surplus of productive industry; whatever is a charge on industry, is a very important diminution of the fund for that sustenance; for the profits of the farmer being lessened, he would be less able to contribute his share to the rates of the parish; and thus the poor, from the exercise of this supposed right in the autumn, would be liable to starve in the spring.[4]

Under this new order, capitalist agriculture had priority over the land. Areas not cultivated to these standards were liable to be claimed, cleared, and bounded as private property to facilitate their "improvement." This deprived the people of customary rights that facilitated ways of living that persisted across centuries. It is not surprising that this process of enclosure sparked long traditions of resistance and rebellion.

As the pace of evictions increased in the sixteenth century and the ranks of the dispossessed swelled, there was alarm that these vagabonds posed a grave threat to the social order. Enclosure was a primary issue in a wave of popular revolts. Kett's Rebellion in 1549, which saw a band of rebels seize the city of Norwich, began when the people of Wymondham tore down the fences that enclosed formerly common land. Likewise, enclosure triggered the riots that engulfed the Midlands in 1607. Those who participated in this uprising were known as levellers or diggers, because the disturbances were characterised by the levelling of ditches and fences erected by enclosers. Fearing that the social order was being undermined, the monarch tried to limit enclosure, but this was largely ineffective, and across the seventeenth century the expropriation of the land continued apace as the centuries-long power struggle between the monarch and the landholding class erupted into the chaos of the Civil War and the Restoration, and the assertion of the primacy of Parliament—a body of property owners elected by other property owners. The making of property involved a double dispossession. Not only were the people deprived of their customary rights to the land, the monarch was also dispossessed of their divinely ordained ownership of the land. With the legal and political powers of the state at their disposal, the propertied class articulated a radically new property order, in which the expropriation of land to create private property was a natural right and moral duty.

These understandings developed hand in hand with patterns of colonisation. Thomas More's satire *Utopia*, published in 1516, reveals the kinds of thinking that were emergent in this period. In a time of heightened fears about the ranks of dispossessed roaming England, More proposed that Utopia should export its surplus population abroad to somewhere where people had more land than they could cultivate. Ideally, the settler and indigenous societies would work together for the common good, but if the indigenous population resisted, it was "a very just cause of war, for a nation to hinder others from possessing a part of that soil of which they make no use of, but which is suffered to lie idle and uncultivated; since every man has by the law of nature a right to such a waste portion of the earth."[5] This belief that land deemed uncultivated could be claimed with force lay at the heart of the English imperial project.

Ireland was the first country subjected to this form of colonisation. Following the Norman invasion, control of Ireland was entrusted to a smattering of English warlords, but this system of governance failed to pacify Ireland. After a wave of rebellion in the sixteenth century, control was extended by driving the Irish from the land and establishing "plantations" of English and Scottish settlers. Sir John Davies, architect of the plantations, justified this expropriation by arguing that though the land was inhabited, "half their land doth now lie waste, by reason whereof that which is habited is not improved to half the value." The Irish, he argued, were incapable of improving the land whereas settlers will ensure that "500 acres will be of better value than 5000 are now."[6] The justification of colonisation therefore prompted new articulations of both property and value that legitimated not only the expropriation of unoccupied land, but any land that was not "improved" to the standards of intensified English agriculture. The Plantations unsurprisingly failed to pacify Ireland. In 1641, the Irish rebelled against the new property order and seized control of more than two-thirds of Ireland. The Civil War delayed English intervention, but in 1649 Oliver Cromwell's army was deployed to restore order. They did so with the utmost brutality, killing somewhere in the region of 20 percent of the population. In the aftermath, the Irish were ordered to leave their lands and relocate west of the Shannon. Their land was apportioned amongst those who had financed and fought in the invasion.

Justifications for the colonisation of America were similar to those deployed in Ireland. John Winthrop, a leading figure in the Massachusetts Bay Colony, reassured potential settlers that they could rightfully claim the new lands. He argued that the command in Genesis to "increase and multiply, replenish the earth and subdue it" gave man two forms of rights over the land: an original natural right to the land and a superior civil right derived from cultivation. Because the indigenous population "inclose noe land neither have any settled habitation nor any tame cattle to improve the land," Winthrop argued, they had only a natural right to the land, "soe as if we leave them sufficient for their use wee many lawfully take the rest."[7] The proviso that sufficient land was left was soon forgotten as it became clear how profitable appropriation of the land was.

In addition to the usual violent forms of expropriation, colonisers turned to economic and legal methods of dispossession. Mortgages were developed in medieval England as a way around the prohibition of usury. Rather than deriving profit from interest payments, lenders used a *gage* that entitled them to the rents and fruits of the debtor's land until the loan was repaid. Gages were either living, meaning that income derived from the land was used to repay the loan, or dead—the *mort* gage—where proceeds from the land were kept as profit rather than deducted from the outstanding loan. Unsurprisingly, the mortgage quickly became popular. In time, lenders gained increased rights over the land to secure the debt, but in England it remained exceedingly difficult and expensive to legally repossess the land in the event of nonpayment.[8] In America, the law was less forgiving of debtors when, as K-Sue Park highlights, credit became integral to conquest. Park shows how foreclosure was developed as a tool of dispossession and the ways in which "debt created through colonial lending practices, often predatory in nature, enabled the seizure of indigenous land." John Pynchon became one of Massachusetts's largest landowners in this way. He allowed the Norworrock Sachem Umpanchela to acquire goods such as coats, breeches, and cotton on credit from his store, sold at a far higher price than he charged European settlers. To settle the £75 debt, Umpanchela was forced to mortgage most of the land to Pynchon, bar some fields reserved for the tribe's use. Pynchon quickly foreclosed on this land and just months later, we learn the tribe's remaining land had been mortgaged for three coats and four yards of cloth, and was subsequently foreclosed by Pynchon.[9]

The colonies established on expropriated land were hierarchical property orders. Although the precise form varied between settlements, property making was integral to the process of state building. In 1663, Charles II granted rights to a group known as the Lord Proprietors to make a colony in the Carolinas. To establish the new state, the Proprietors needed settlers to defend the territory and generate tax revenue. They used the promise of land ownership and political rights to tempt potential migrants. The landscape was mapped and divided into uniform acre plots, which were sold at £3 each, with title guaranteed by a land register. New owners were offered differing political rights according to the acreage purchased: 12,000 acres made the owner a baron with control over local government, 3,000 acres made a manorial lord with rights to administer justice, while 50 acres gave the purchaser the right to vote. Labourers also needed to be attracted to work the land, therefore a further 150 acres of land was granted for each labourer or slave imported.[10] The creation of property rights therefore went hand in hand with the creation of the new state the colonists moulded in the image of England: a hierarchical property order where structures of law and governance were dominated by property owners.

The ideas developed through colonisation shaped English property relations. John Locke formed his understanding of property while serving as secretary to the Proprietors of Carolina, a position he secured thanks to his patron Lord Shaftesbury, who was one of the Proprietors. Locke's *Treatise of Government* did not so much propose a new theory of property as it articulated the ways of thinking that had emerged through practices of enclosure and colonisation. He sought to demonstrate how private property rights could be acquired given that the earth was originally bequeathed to man in common. Like More, Davies, and Winthrop, Locke looked to cultivation, improvement, and labour to justify this expropriation. He began his argument with a series of metaphors about common rights. He asked the reader to consider the commoner eating fruit gathered from the woods and questions, "When did they begin to be his? When he digested? Or when he ate? Or when he boiled? Or when he brought them home? Or when he picked them up?" Locke argued that ownership began when the commoner exerted labour to gather the fruit:

> Every man has a "property" in his own "person." This nobody has any right to but himself. The "labour" of his body and the "work" of his hands, we may say, are properly his. Whatsoever, then, he removes out of the state that Nature hath

provided and left it in, he hath mixed his labour with it, and joined to it something that is his own, and thereby makes it his property.[11]

Locke argued that what held for fruit holds for land: "As much land as a
man tills, plants, improves, cultivates, and can use the product of, so much is
his property. He by his labour does, as it were, enclose from the common."
Such action did not necessitate the consent of the commoners as long as there
was still enough land to go around. Locke conceded this was not possible in
England, but reassured the reader that as "full as the world seems," if you
gazed beyond England to the colonisable world, and to America in particular, "there are still great tracts of ground to be found, which the inhabitants
thereof . . . lie waste, and are more than the people who dwell on it, do, or can
make use of, and so still lie in common." Like others before, he argued that
the indigenous peoples of America had no claim to the land as they had not
cultivated and improved it. Locke compared an acre of industriously farmed
English land with an acre of American land. With the right application of
labour, both could generate equivalent value, but as it is, "the benefit mankind
receives from one in a year is worth five pounds, and the other possibly not
worth a penny."[12] Expropriation would therefore collectively benefit human-
kind. In this way Locke justified the expropriation of any land that was not
as profitable as the most intensively farmed land in England in the name of
the common good.

Locke advanced a slightly different argument to justify the theft of common land in England, given he conceded there was insufficient land for it to
be appropriated without doing harm to others. He claimed that common land
in England was not common to mankind in general, only "common in respect
of some men": those who collectively owned it thanks to a grant from time
immemorial. Locke here occasioned a subtle but significant shift, displacing
the idea of common rights with common ownership. According to this logic,
commoners did not in themselves possess the right to use the land, rather
these rights were acquired because at some point in a mythical past, the
community was given the land. Therefore, if the descendants of this bequest
consented, land could be enclosed and converted into private property.[13]
Following Locke, the commons were radically redefined from something that
people had the right to use, to spaces that were collectively owned and could
be privatised in the name of improvement and agricultural efficiency.

As Locke's ideas gained a readership in the eighteenth century, this logic
formed the basis for Parliamentary Enclosure, which codified the ad hoc processes of the last centuries. Under this system, an individual could petition
Parliament, setting out the advantages to be gained from enclosure and dem-
onstrating they had the support of at least two-thirds of landholders. A private
bill then had to pass through both the House of Commons and the Lords,

making enclosure slow and expensive. In the mid-nineteenth century, the process was rationalized with the introduction of an Inclosure Commission. Owners representing one-third of the *value* of the land could initiate the process by completing a form and setting out the advantages anticipated. The common land would then be divided between the landholders as bounded private property. Although the commission greatly rationalized the process of enclosure, the principals underlying both stages of Parliamentary Enclosure were the same.

The justification for enclosure was invariably "improvement," and as Locke had reasoned, this was characterised as being in the public good. The process itself extinguished customary rights. Echoing Locke's characterisation, Parliamentary Enclosure was based on the fiction of the collective ownership of the commons rather than the traditional and popular understanding of land as governed by customary rights and unbounded by notions of exclusive ownership. This fiction meant that Parliament acknowledged only those perceived to have a legal claim to the land; those whose subsistence depended on customary rights exercised for generations were of no account. A simple majority was enough to dispossess whole communities. The terms of the Inclosure Commission, which required only the consent of landholders representing a third of the value of the land, placed power and control of the landscape in the hands of large and wealthy landholders. This was an issue long before the more favourable terms of the Inclosure Commission, as Mary Houghton's case demonstrates.

Mary's case was about much more than just gleaning. The Houghtons owned a cottage with common rights on the Cornwallis estate in Suffolk. These rights enabled the family to sustain a fragile independence; unlike many others in the village, in the decades before the prosecution, there is no evidence that they had applied for parish relief.[14] Across the eighteenth century, the Cornwallis estate progressively bought up land in the parish and by 1780 owned virtually all of Timworth, bar a few freeholdings, including the Houghtons. Cornwallis was keen to fully enclose the village but was obstructed by the Houghtons, who were understandably keen not to lose their vital rights over the land. However, following the case and hefty fine, the Houghtons fell into debt and were twice forced to mortgage their property before finally auctioning it in 1796. This removed the last obstacle to the enclosure of the estate, and the land was appropriated months later. Mary was widowed shortly after she lost her home, and the last trace of her is in the poor law records, propertyless and dependent on parish relief.[15] The Houghton case was remarkable only in the trace it left in the historic record. The removal of seemingly small customary rights, such as gleaning, had a devastating impact on the fragile subsistence economy of the rural poor. E. P. Thompson describes enclosure as:

a plain enough case of class robbery, played according to the fair rules of
property and law laid down by a parliament of property-owners and lawyers.
. . . What was "perfectly proper" in terms of capitalist property-relations
involved, none the less, a rupture of the traditional integument of village custom
and of right: and the social violence of enclosure consisted precisely in the dras-
tic total imposition upon the village of capitalist property-definitions.[16]

Through the process of enclosure, the property-owning class deployed their
institutions of Parliament and law to dispossess the people of their customary rights, extinguishing ways of living that had persisted for centuries and
rendering the landless poor totally dependent upon wage labour to meet their
most basic needs. Parliamentary Enclosure codified the understandings of
property that gestated in England and Empire over several centuries, but
now, as law, the idea of exclusive private property was exported as a universal truth, as a means of possessing new territories and extending control
over existing colonies. The Houghton case speaks to this interconnectedness
of enclosure and empire building. Earl Cornwallis, upon whose estate Mary
lived, was appointed Governor General of India in 1786. He was tasked with
quelling mounting resistance and rebellion and addressing the need for a
more efficient way to extract revenue. The way to bring order to the region,
Cornwallis thought, was to impose the English system of property relations.
In the years in which Mary was being persecuted on his estate in Suffolk,
Cornwallis devised the Permanent Settlement of Bengal, which extinguished
the rights of those who cultivated the land and anointed as landlords the
zamindars, a class who previously had the right to collect revenues from the
land but were in no way owners.[17] The new landlords sought to extract ever
increasing amounts of rent from the land. By the 1870s, rents stood at four
or five times the level they were at the time of the settlement. This forced
tenants to cultivate cash crops, such as indigo and cotton, rather than the rice
and wheat they needed to subsist, contributing to the recurrent famines that
afflicted the region in the nineteenth century. Rising rents fuelled a wave of
unrest that spread in the 1870s from Pabna, where villages refused to pay rent
or recognise the property claims of landlords, eventually declaring independence and setting up their own government and rebel army.[18] The clear failure
of the settlement, and of other colonial property orders, in conjunction with
the dangers posed by the expansion of the franchise, forced a remaking of
property for the democratic age.

THE CHALLENGE OF DEMOCRACY

Property making dispossessed people of their basic means of subsistence and contravened popular notions of justice. It not only provoked acts of resistance in the moment but animated popular radicalism over centuries. As Alun Howkins has shown, "Generation after generation of working men and women, urban as well as rural, persisted in the belief that the land, or more accurately its ownership and control, was not an issue of minor importance, but was central to human life and politics." Although the form of radicalism varied over time, what was shared "was a belief that the land had been taken from its rightful owners the people."[19] What was distinct about this tradition in the late nineteenth century was its articulation within parliamentary politics.

The 1867 Representation of the People Act enfranchised sections of the urban working class. It was assumed this would benefit the Liberals, but they lost ground on the side to a jingoistic Conservatism that promised to defend beer, gambling and pleasure from the Liberals' moralising grasp, and on the other, to the emergence of working class political organisations.[20] So when the act was extended to the countryside in 1884, Liberals could not be complacent. In a series of inflammatory speeches in the run up to the 1885 election, Joseph Chamberlain sought to woo the newly enfranchised by tapping into popular anger about enclosure. The people, he declared, had a natural right to the land, but their rights had been "given away by people who had no right to dispose of them," "stolen by fraud" or "acquired by violence." The only thing that stands in the way of "men who would make very short work of private ownership" is the state. Society must therefore ask itself: "What ransom will property pay for the security which it enjoys? What substitute will it find for the natural rights which have ceased to be recognized?"[21]

Chamberlain's bombastic rhetoric shocked the establishment, but it was a shrewd political move calculated to appeal to a number of different constituencies. He delivered this speech not to rural workers, but to an urban audience in Birmingham. He reminded them that displaced agricultural labourers are "driven into towns to compete with you for work and to lower the rate of wages" leaving the labouring population "huddled into dwellings unfit for man or beast, where the conditions of common decency are impossible, and where they lead directly to disease, intemperance, and crime."[22] Such a rhetoric was designed to appeal not just to the working classes but also to the anxious middle class who looked on aghast at the growth of the city. As Gareth Steadman Jones argues:

> In the late 1860s and early 1870s, the liberal utopia had never seemed nearer. The bulk of the middle and upper classes had never felt more secure or confident in the future. But there remained the slight but disturbing possibility that the

forces of progress might be swamped by the corrupting features of urban life, that, unless checked or reformed, the "residuum" might overrun the newly built citadel of moral virtue and economic rationality.[23]

Rural resettlement promised to undo the harms of the city. These ideas had circulated within Liberal thought since the midcentury. 1848 saw the publication of W. T. Thornton's *A Plea for Peasant Proprietors* and J. S. Mill's *Principles of Political Economy*. Both argued that peasant proprietorship cultivated good moral character, "a sort of magic power of engendering industry, perseverance and forethought."[24] Thornton stressed the social stability ownership induced:

> A mere day-labourer, half employed, and wretchedly paid . . . not unnaturally regards his employers as oppressors, takes every opportunity of showing his spite by wanton aggressions, and is ever ready to listen to the harangues of seditious demagogues. But a peasant proprietor has no such cause for envy or animosity against the owners of larger estates, but is rather disposed to join with them in repelling any attack on their common rights.[25]

Published as a wave of revolutionary unrest swept across Europe, these ideas had immediate appeal. Although revolt did not spread to Britain, fear of contagion was always present, particularly from the 1860s, when the economic downturn triggered a series of riots in Britain's urban centres.[26] The publication of the New Doomsday survey in 1876 focused public attention on the distribution of property. It revealed that a quarter of the land was owned by just 710 families.[27] Emile de Laveleye warned of the particular danger Britain found itself in now that the propertyless were enfranchised: "The concentration of land in large estates among a small number of families is a sort of provocation of levelling legislative measures." He called for the creation of a class of peasant proprietors to form "a kind of rampart and safeguard for the holders of large estates."[28] While the defence of a limited franchise had rested upon the idea that only those with property had the character to vote responsibly, as ever more of the people gained the right to vote, Liberals argued that a redistribution of property was necessary to safeguard the existing order and promote the moral character of the newly enfranchised through the "magic of property."

Chamberlain's critique of property aimed to appeal to both the working and middle classes. By creating a cross-class alliance against the traditional Tory landowning sect, Chamberlain hoped to see off the threat posed by working class politics and secure a future for the Liberal Party in the democratic age. Although his rhetoric was inflammatory, his proposals sat comfortably within the Liberal tradition in calling for some redistribution of property through market mechanisms. Indeed, the "ransom" Chamberlain demanded was for local authorities to be given powers to purchase allotments and smallholdings as a form of restitution for the theft of the land. By the end of the century, far bolder solutions to the land question came to the fore as a new generation of Liberals questioned the institution of property itself.

J. S. Mill, who was the MP for City and Westminster in the 1860s, was central to this development. His critique of property emerged through his reflections on imperial governance. Observing the different understandings of property at play across the Empire, he argued that English ideas about of property were "not universal at all, but merely English customs."[29] Mill's interest in India was kindled at a young age via the teachings of his father, who in the year of Mill's birth began writing a history of Britain in India. His thoughts developed during the thirty-five years in which he worked for the East India Company. He believed one of the gravest errors made in India was the Permanent Settlement of Bengal, where, in their haste to make English landlords, "it proved that they had only created Irish ones."[30] Later settlements, which took greater account of customary rights, were an advance, as they demonstrated a "perception of recognition of its differences from England." Mill urged, "What has been done for India now has to be done for Ireland."[31]

Mill accused the English of making the same mistake in Ireland as they had in India by imposing ideas of property without regard for Irish custom, under which "the right to hold the land goes, as it did in the beginning, with the right to till."[32] Since the 1840s, Parliament had sought to reorganise Irish agriculture in the image of England, abolishing customary rights and imposing contractual law. Mill called for them to change tack and legislate "according to Irish exigencies and no longer according to English routine," restating tenants' permanent rights over the land.[33] He warned of the consequences of not reforming property order. Nothing would prevent Fenianism "being the standing torment of the English Government and people" until the underlying grievance was tackled: the imposition of the English belief in absolute property in land. He accused the English of conceit in their institutions and challenged the historical and moral justification of absolute property in land: "a thing which no man made, which exists in limited quantity, which was the original inheritance of all mankind and which, whoever appropriates, keeps others out of its possession."[34] This shocked the establishment. The *Times* treated the text to three days of comment. It compared Mill's ideas to Pierre-Joseph Proudhon's pronouncement that property was theft and warned of the grave implications of such a scheme:

Every man should make up his mind whether the received laws of property are to be upheld in the United Kingdom; or whether, beginning first with Ireland, we are to establish principals which would unsettle our whole social fabric. . . . The first thing to be borne in mind is that every theory accepted for Ireland is accepted for England.[35]

Mill was fully aware of the implications of his ideas in England. He described the English property order as "the remains of a system which, as history tells us, was designed to prop up a ruling class."[36] While more moderate Liberals placed faith in the unfettered market to bring about an equitable distribution of property, Mill doubted the allocative justice of the market: "As long as the private wealth of this country and its social condition are what they are, the rich will always outbid the poor in the land market."[37] Moreover, for Mill, land was not simply another form of commodity: "No man made the land. It is the original inheritance of the whole species."[38] Urbanisation exposed the issues with Lockean theories of property, which justified property in land on the basis of labour. Over the course of the nineteenth century, the value of urban land increased dramatically. The rateable value of the City of London rose from £1,332,092 in 1861 to £3,479,428 in 1881.[39] Such increases owed little to the labour of the owner but derived from the collective provision of the infrastructure necessary to sustain urban life. Mill asked, "What have the possessors done, that this increase of wealth produced by other people's labour and enterprise, should fall into their mouths as they sleep, instead of being applied to the public necessities of those who created it?"[40] A tax on this "unearned increment" would ensure that the "increase of wealth which now flows into the coffers of private persons from the mere progress of society, and not from their own merits or sacrifices, will be gradually, and in an increasing proportion, diverted from them to the nation as a whole, from whose collective exertions and sacrifices it really proceeds."[41] Such proposals were too much for moderate Liberal opinion, and Mill was struck off the Cobden Club's Committee for having "publicly identified himself with principals radically opposed to those of Cobden"[42]

Surprisingly little time elapsed before Mill's proposals became Liberal policy. Continued disorder in Ireland was one factor that drove this shift. In 1867, the Irish Republican Brotherhood (IRB) led a failed uprising in Ireland. This was obviously unsettling for the English, but hardly unprecedented. What worried the authorities more was the potential of this disorder to spread to England. In December 1867, the IRB staged a prison break at Clerkenwell. Due to their inexperience, they overestimated the explosives needed, and not only destroyed the prison wall, but the tenement houses opposite, killing 12 and injuring a further 120. The *Times* warned that there were "still among us others planning outrages equally dastardly and deadly, and that any day may bring some disastrous news."[43] Disastrous news was to come the following year from Tipperary. When the murder of a policeman and a bailiff hit the English press, there was outrage. However, as details of the case began to emerge, the press were forced to take a more nuanced line. The land at Ballycohey had changed hands frequently in recent decades, but the arrival of William Scully was viewed with particular apprehension. He owned large estates across Ireland and America and was renowned for forcefully asserting his property rights. In the 1840s, he was tried and acquitted of shooting two sons of a tenant he was trying to evict; in 1865, he was sentenced to a year's hard labour for beating the wife of another tenant who crossed his path. When he arrived at Ballycohey, he tried to force the tenants to accept harsh new leases, but the tenants had other ideas. Every time Scully tried to serve the notices, the tenants abandoned their houses, which the community defended. However, on one occasion Scully and the police and bailiffs accompanying him tried to force their way through a demonstration and were greeted by a volley of shots which struck four of the party, including Scully. In the aftermath, rather than condemn the actions of the tenants, local dignitaries defended their character. One of Scully's relative's, Carbery Scully, testified that the tenants were "the most honest, quiet, and industrious people I ever met."[44] Even the *Times* placed the blame for the incident firmly on Scully for attempting to impose such ruthless leases and endangering the lives of police in the process. The tenants, it concluded, "were subjected to gross provocation, and took a murderous revenge."[45] Not only was the landed order a persistent cause of Irish disorder, the ruthlessness and violence of the system in practice was becoming indefensible.

When the Liberals were returned to power, they attempted to appease the Irish situation with radical land reform. Introducing the 1870 Landlord and Tenant Act, Prime Minister William Gladstone argued that while property might be commonsense in England and Scotland, in Ireland,

> where the old Irish ideas and customs were never supplanted except by the rude hand of violence and by laws written on the Statute Book, but never entering into the heart of the Irish people—the people have not generally embraced the idea of the occupation of land by contract; and the old Irish notion that some interest in the soil adheres to the tenant . . . is everywhere rooted in the popular mind.[46]

The 1870 and 1881 Land Acts gave the "Ulster Custom" the force of law across Ireland. This recognised tenants' property in land by giving them the right to sell their tenancy. For more traditional Liberals, this system of dual ownership was an intolerable transgression of the property order, and the passing of these acts exacerbated tensions within the party. Despite the high political cost, the acts did little to quell the situation in Ireland, where the provisions were overtaken by events. The agricultural depression of the 1870s prompted a renewed wave of evictions. During the 1880s, the Land League organised a sustained campaign against these evictions and Ireland once again became increasingly ungovernable. Trying to find a solution, Gladstone introduced a Home Rule Bill in 1886. This was a step too far for many in the party, and the Liberal Unionists crossed the floor and joined the Conservative benches. This new political formation would have a long-lasting impact on British politics.

The departure of the traditional wing of the party enabled the Liberals to embrace a range of radical social policies, especially regarding ownership of the land. The success of the Conservative appeal to the urban working class and the rise of Labour meant that from the 1880s the Liberals became more reliant on the vote of the rural working class.[47] The problem was that Joseph Chamberlain was one of those who defected to the Conservatives, taking his schemes for allotments and small holdings with him. Among the people, far more radical proposals were being discussed. Particularly influential were the ideas of Henry George, which he set out in *Poverty and Progress* (1879), one of the best-selling books of the age. His ideas circulated far beyond the page. Groups such as the Land Nationalisation Society and the Land Restoration League toured rural England in little yellow and red vans, disseminating George's radical ideas about land and property, while in the city, George addressed large public rallies.[48] George argued that the reason poverty persisted amid so much progress and advancing wealth was not "competition; it does not result from any inevitable conflict between labour and capital; it is not a legitimate outgrowth of the wages system. It is simply the inevitable result of making that element necessary to all men the private property of some men."[49] George described the enclosure of the land as the one "great wrong" from which all social evils derived. The restoration of people's right to the land did not, however, require a literal redistribution of land; rather, the people could enact their right to the land by collecting rents from the current occupiers in the form of taxation.

The popularity of George's ideas in both urban and rural Britain meant there was a political advantage to be derived from articulating land taxation as Liberal policy, but there were also economic justifications for its adoption. It promised to solve the crisis in local taxation. The cost of public works and social welfare fell largely on local taxpayers. Taxes were paid by the occupier, not the owner, so the bill for urban investment fell disproportionately on the working and lower middle classes. Gladstone rallied against the inequity of a system in which improvements were built not "at the expense of the permanent proprietary interests" but "upon the wages of the labouring man in fuel necessary for his family."[50] Local taxation increased rapidly towards the end of the century, rising on average by 141 percent between 1875 and 1900, exacting a heavy political cost on Liberal councils who tried to alleviate conditions in their cities.[51] Land taxation, which would shift the burden of urban improvements onto landowners, was therefore appealing. It was introduced in 1909, as part of Lloyd George's People's Budget, which proposed a range of revenue-generating measures to try and square the circle between his ambitious programme of social reform and the rising cost of rearmament.

Like Mill and Henry George, Lloyd George proposed taxing the unearned increment, the increase in land value that derived from the effort of the community. This was based on the idea that land was not in any sense absolutely owned; the landowner and the community both had possession in the land. Such an idea was an anathema to the landowning class, who dominated the political system. The House of Lords rejected the finance bill, triggering a constitutional crisis, the general elections of 1910 and the abolition of the House of Lords' powers of veto. Before the tax could be implemented, war interjected. Despite Lloyd George's attempt to revive the issue in the 1920s, land taxation retreated from the political agenda as the influence of the Liberal Party permanently waned.

THE PROPERTY-OWNING DEMOCRACY

For Conservatives and former Liberals, land taxation transgressed the bounds of tolerable political debate. The British political system was, after all, a hierarchical property order designed to sustain the dominance of a small landowning class. To suggest, as the Liberals were, that the making of property was illegitimate was to throw into question the very foundations of the entire legal and political order. Although the Conservatives' first instinct was to defend the existing property order and the interests of the landed classes, such a strategy was no longer tenable in the democratic age. Instead, they conceded to some redistribution of property to preserve the institution of property itself.

This might appear a dramatic departure for the Conservatives, but it needs to be understood in the context of the declining importance of land to their traditional supporters. The value of land declined from a peak of £2 billion in the late 1870s to just £1.155 billion in 1914. While land values halved, industrial and commercial assets rose by 300 percent.[52] During this period, the landed classes diversified their assets, making the most of new overseas investment opportunities.[53] The aristocracy also entered the world of business and finance, and by the 1890s, half the peerage were company directors while a quarter of partners in London's leading merchant banking houses were married to daughters of peers.[54] Conservative debates about land reform therefore occurred in a period in which land became less important to their core vote.

There was also political capital to be made from a new land policy. Before the final split in 1886, Conservatives sought to exploit the tensions brewing among Liberals over the question of property. In 1883, Conservative leader Lord Salisbury argued that a new form of radicalism verging on socialism now dominated the Liberal party. He pitied traditional Liberals forced to watch their party treat values such as "individual freedom and the sacredness of property . . . as matters of a very light account"[55] Salisbury was prepared to make concessions to persuade moderate Liberals that when it came to questions of property, they were in agreement. In 1885, he proposed abolishing the set of hereditary customs that prevented the free sale of landed estates, something Liberals had long campaigned for and which Conservatives had always opposed. This was not indicative of any ideological conversion, rather it was an exercise in practical politics, as he explained to Randolph Churchill:

> The abolition of primogeniture is in itself of no importance except on strategic grounds—it is not worth the trouble of resistance. But it is a bit of a flag. The concession would be distasteful to a certain number of our people now, and it might be acceptable as a wedding present to the Moderate Liberals whenever the Conservative party leads them to the alter.[56]

Salisbury did not have to wait long. Just a few months later, the Liberals split over Home Rule. Not only did many moderates cross the floor, but they were joined by Radicals, including Chamberlain. A commitment to land reform was vital to maintain this fragile coalition and confine the new and dangerous Liberalism to the peripheries. By coming out in favour of free trade in land and incorporating Chamberlain's proposals for allotments and smallholdings (albeit without compulsory purchasing powers), Conservatives adopted moderate Liberal policies to affect a redistribution of property via the free market.

Conservatives justified these policies through Liberal tropes. They were deeply apprehensive about the consequences of democratisation and looked to the magic of property to shore up the existing order. As Henry Chaplin explained:

> It is an entire mistake to suppose that the Tory Party . . . are in any degree whatever opposed to a large distribution of land among the people of this country. . . . I wish to see a large addition to the owners of land in this country, because land is no longer the same safe kind of property that it used to be . . . a large increase in the number of owners of land such as I desire is, I think, the surest and perhaps the only safeguard against the predatory instincts of a class whose Socialistic schemes have found such powerful exponents in these days.[57]

The socialist threat was a prominent theme in Conservative politics from the 1880s. Used somewhat vaguely, it was a catchall term for any interference with property rights which sought to benefit the propertyless at the expense of the propertied.[58] The idea that only a democratisation of property ownership could safeguard the existing order gained traction within the Conservative Party at the turn of the century. Justifying the provision of allotments and smallholdings, Salisbury admitted that it wast not the most efficient means of food production, but "there are things more important than economy. I believe that a small proprietary constitutes the strongest bulwark against revolutionary change, and afford the soundest support for the Conservative feeling and institutions of the country."[59] This idea would become one of key pillars of twentieth-century British Conservatism, but it was in Ireland that it would have the greatest immediate impact.

In the 1880s, Conservatives inherited a situation in Ireland they found abhorrent. The Liberal Land Acts established a system of dual ownership antithetical to the universalism of English property law. The least objectionable part of the legislation for the Tories were the Bright clauses, which empowered the state to lend tenants two thirds of the cost of land purchase. This was largely ineffective, as very few tenants had the means to raise the deposit, and by 1887 just 731 tenants had purchased land under the clauses.[60] As the agricultural depression deepened, poverty, evictions and agitation gripped the Irish countryside. Further land reform appeared necessary to preserve the union. The Conservatives perceived an opportunity to tackle what Arthur Balfour, the Chief Secretary to Ireland, termed the "abomination" of the 1881 Land Act. The only final solution, he told Salisbury, was purchase.[61] Not only did this promise to quell unrest, but through widespread land purchase they might lead Ireland back to the English system of individual ownership. Successive Land Purchase Acts between 1885 and 1903 provided tenants with loans for the full purchase of land on generous terms, calculated to ensure that the cost of purchase was less than rent. This was not a bad deal for landlords. Rent controls and the loss of individual and absolute ownership rights, not to mention persistent unrest, rendered land in Ireland practical unsaleable. In this context, the offer to buy land at full market value looked generous, particularly if the alternative might be forcible expropriation. By 1919, nearly half of all agricultural land had been sold to tenants.[62] Through these acts, Conservatives effected a tenurial revolution in Ireland in which individual and absolute property rights prevailed.

In England, the politics of property became increasingly important to Conservatives following their humiliating defeat of 1906, which ended twenty years of Conservative dominance and left the party with its lowest ever number of MPs. Land taxation was a key issue at this election and the Liberal landslide suggested the policy was popular. When Lloyd George announced his intention to introduce land taxes in 1909, Conservatives went on the offensive. While Liberals argued that property in land was distinct from other forms of property, Conservatives strove to present Liberal policies as a threat to property in general. Speaking to a packed hall in Birmingham, Balfour, now party leader, rallied against Lloyd George's "slipshod socialism." He warned the crowd that "you cannot isolate one form of property from another." If the budget passed, there would be nothing to stop the state from confiscating anything else acquired through "enterprise and thrift."[63] Popular propaganda emphasised the threat this posed to every home and family. As Jon Lawrence has argued, "Conservatives appropriated the sentimental vocabulary of Victorian domesticity to provide the cornerstones of a new Tory discourse of anti-socialism."[64] A Primrose League pamphlet, for example, argued that socialism was a threat to the "every-Englishman's-house-is-his-castle system" which "may be ever so humble" but is the "no-place-like-home system."[65] Conservatives pledged they would not only defend the property of existing owners, but enable more people to become owners. Balfour pointed to what they had achieved in Ireland and promised that, if elected, the Conservatives would oversee "a great extension of such ownership to England. Nothing could be more desirable or important."[66]

The Conservatives were not, however, returned to government until the 1920s. It was in this decade that the term the *property-owning democracy* was first coined. In 1923, Noel Skelton published a series of articles in which he set forth his vision for a *Constructive Conservatism*. He was a key figure in the development twentieth-century Conservatism. Although he died in 1935, those who coalesced around him went on to define Conservative politics in the postwar period. Skelton was regarded as the intellectual leader of a grouping, known derisively as the YMCA, that included future leaders Anthony Eden, Harold MacMillan and Alec Douglas-Home. In 1923, Skelton warned that the fate of Conservatism hung in the balance. It had been presented a unique opportunity to shape "the national destiny at the very beginning of a new political era," but among the electorate the appeal of socialism was growing.[67] Skelton believed the people to be instinctively Conservative and that the popularity of socialism was indicative of a failure to positively articulate a Conservative vision of the future. He called on Conservatives to make "clear to the nation that it, too, has a vision of the future. Of a property-owning democracy."[68]

Property ownership, Skelton argued, strengthened the broader tenets of Conservatism, social stability and strength of individual character: "For what is the effect of property, its proverbial 'magic'? In the getting, the exercise of thrift, of control, of all the qualities which 'the rolling-stone' knows nothing of; in its use, an increased-sense of responsibility, a wider economic outlook, a practical medium for the expression of moral and intellectual qualities." As well as the "vital inter-relation between character and private possessions" was the "relation between the possession of private property by the people and the stability of the State." This was long appreciated by Conservatism:

> In the past it was wont to maintain that only those who possessed private property should exercise political functions. That doctrine has now this new and pregnant application—that since, to-day, practically all citizens have political rights, all should possess something of their own. Mocked and jeered at in the past as "the Party of Property," it is precisely as such, now that the wheel has turned full circle, that Conservatism in the new era holds in its keeping the key to the problem.[69]

Through the magic of property, Skelton aspired to create Conservative subjects and starve socialism of its popular support. His vision of a property-owning democracy was not simply about homeownership, rather a broader plan encompassing industrial co-partnership, small ownership in land and agricultural cooperation. When these ideas were translated through the politics of Prime Minister Stanley Baldwin, they acquired a more domestic emphasis.

For Baldwin, homeownership was the solution to the key instability of the age: that war had brought "a fully-fledged democracy before we are ready for it." His main duty as Prime Minister was to "educate a new democracy . . . and make them realise their responsibilities in their possession of power."[70] Baldwin looked to the magic of property to perform this educative function. The aspiration to homeownership was "a stimulus to one's self-respect and one's independence."[71] It was precisely these sorts of values that would inoculate the population against socialism and help the nation endure the democratic age: "If you want a lasting democracy you must have a property-owning democracy."[72] Baldwin's government legislated to stimulate homeownership. The 1923 Housing Act diverted subsidies away from the nascent council house programme towards the construction of homes for sale. As well as subsidising house building, it also empowered councils to help with housing finance, either by providing mortgages directly or by guaranteeing building society loans. Under the act, £23.5 million was spent subsidising 362,200 dwellings and £724 million advanced as mortgages.[73]

Although far from insignificant, the act was not in itself responsible for the rapid growth in homeownership in the interwar years. Far more important, as later chapters show, was the collapse of the private rental sector and the greater availability of housing finance.[74] But this did not stop the government taking credit for the growth. Baldwin declared that Conservative housing policy was "the greatest success that any Government in a similar line has ever achieved."[75] Like his Edwardian predecessors, Baldwin sought to associate Conservativism with images of domesticity and home. On the day of his appointment as Prime Minister, the press was invited to Chequers to capture images of Baldwin, pipe in hand, relaxing in the garden with his family.[76] He keenly understood the new forms of politics ushered in by the advent of radio. During the 1924 election, while H. H. Asquith and Ramsay MacDonald broadcast from public rallies, Baldwin appreciated the more intimate tone required and spoke from the BBC offices, occasionally puffing from his pipe, while his wife knitted in the background.[77] In later speeches he emphasised the domestic intimacy of the medium, noting that "I have been talking to you in your own homes as if I were with you there—those homes that mean so much to us all"[78]—homes that were, according to Conservative propaganda, directly threatened by the prospect of a Labour government.

Little adjustment was needed to turn the accusations that Baldwin's predecessors had levelled against the Liberals to attack Labour. A pamphlet produced in 1924 featured a newly built suburban home and promised "Yours! But not under Socialism. . . . If the Socialists have their way, we shall all have to live in State or Council houses, paying rent all the time and never having a home of our own."[79] A poster from 1929 emphasised the threat socialism posed to private life. Subtitled "an Englishman's Home," it featured a modest house encircled by "inspectors" poking their noses in.[80] By promising to defend the sanctity and autonomy of each man's castle from socialism's grasp, the party sought to secure an enduring antisocialist constituent by encouraging actual and aspirant homeowners to identify their interests with the Conservatives.

This rhetoric was deployed against Labour following their landmark victory in 1945. At the first Conservative conference following their humiliating defeat, deputy leader Anthony Eden attempted to rally the party: "The defeat we sustained last year, grievous as it was, is in this respect a blessing, because it gives us an opportunity to redefine our faith and our political objectives." He called on the party to unite around a single principle that he believed best differentiated the ideology of Conservativism from the socialism of Labour:

> The objective of Socialism is state ownership of all the means of production, distribution and exchange. Our objective is a nation-wide property-owning democracy. These objectives are fundamentally opposed. Whereas the Socialist purpose is the concentration of ownership in the hands of the State, ours is the distribution of ownership over the widest practicable number of individuals. . . . Man should be master of his environment and not its slave. That is what freedom means. It is precisely in the conception of ownership that man achieves mastery over his environment. Upon the institution of property depends the fulfilment of individual personality and the maintenance of individual liberty.[81]

Eden was part of the posse associated with Skelton in the interwar period, so it is not surprising that he should turn to his mentor's idea of the property-owning democracy as a rallying call for the defeated party. However, while Skelton had focused on the stabilising force of property ownership to weather the democratic age, Eden spoke more of the freedom and liberty generated by ownership. Freedom was a key trope in postwar Conservativism. In his election broadcast of 1945, Winston Churchill warned that a vote for Labour was a vote for totalitarianism. Socialism, he proclaimed, was "an attack upon the right of the ordinary man or woman to breathe freely without having a harsh, clumsy tyrannical hand clapped across their mouths and nostrils." These arguments were effectively countered by Clement Attlee, who reminded the electorate that the freedom Churchill advocated was merely "freedom for the rich and slavery for the poor." It was only through state action that the people could realise a meaningful freedom.[82] Churchill's misjudged speech is believed to have contributed to the defeat of 1945, and in the late 1940s, Conservatives were preoccupied with how to reconcile freedom with economic security. The idea of the property-owning democracy promised to do just that. Eden pledged that by promoting economic growth, individuals would be able to save, consume and own, gaining economic security free from the state.

Eden's vision of the property-owning democracy was, like Skelton's, about much more than home ownership. Indeed, most of his speech was about partnership in industry, but, as in the interwar period, this wider sense of the property-owning democracy did not resonate with the party, who fixated on the idea of homeownership.[83] Housing, they recognised, was a politically potent issue in the postwar years. Labour was swept to power in 1945 with a bold vision, but by the late 1940s it was clear that the housing programme was a long way behind schedule. It was hampered by shortages of skilled labour and building supplies as the needs of the housing programme were balanced against demands for the reconstruction of industry, education and health. Following the economic crises of 1947, Britain became dependent on US aid and was the largest recipient of funds under the Marshall Plan. The money came with strings attached, and aid continued to flow only because Labour agreed to curtail spending on welfare programmes such as housing.[84] But the housing programme also had to address a problem of enormous proportions. The war considerably exacerbated Britain's housing crisis. Not only did the conflict halt the construction of new houses, nearly half a million houses were destroyed by enemy action. Moreover, after the war there was a rapid growth in households, as marriage rates increased and the baby boomers came into being. Labour's housing programme therefore had to address a shortfall of around 2 million homes, yet in 1947 only 115,000 homes were constructed.[85] All the while, millions of Britons were confined to substandard, overcrowded and shared accommodation. It is not surprising that housing was a key issue for the electorate in these years. In its study of election behaviour in 1945, Mass Observation concluded that "housing was mentioned so often that everything else became by comparison unimportant."[86] Opinion polling suggested that housing remained the most important concern of the electorate throughout the late 1940s.[87] There was clearly potential for Conservatives to make political capital out of the ongoing housing crisis.

During the late 1940s, Conservatives attacked Labour's housing programme. Ignoring the huge challenges of reconstruction, they blamed its failure on Labour's decision to only allow one private house to be built for every four council houses constructed. Churchill claimed this was a "pedantic, irrational enforcement of Socialist prejudice." He promised that Conservatives would end building controls and re-create the kind of housing boom they oversaw in the 1930s.[88] At the 1951 election, the Conservatives promised that by "letting the builder's build," they would deliver 300,000 new houses each year. Socialist controls and regulations, they argued, had "inflicted serious injury upon our strength and prosperity." The issues with the housing programme were, they claimed, indicative of the broader problems with socialism and its failure to provide people with the consumer goods they desired. By releasing private enterprise, the Conservatives promised to usher in a time of "freedom and abundance."[89]

The Conservatives narrowly won the election of 1951, marking the beginning of the end of the social democratic moment in Britain. In their first few years in office, delivering the promised 300,000 houses was a key priority of domestic policy.[90] The target was reached in 1953; however, two-thirds of the homes built that year were council houses.[91] This was not something the government were keen to admit, stressing instead that it was achieved by freeing private enterprise to build. The achievement of the target gave the Conservatives the political space to reorientate policy towards their vision of a property-owning democracy and throughout the late 1950s, they attempted to withdraw the state from the provision and regulation of housing. Rents in the private rented sector were decontrolled, council house building was scaled back, and local authorities were permitted to sell off housing at below market rates. They were also encouraged to make greater use of their power to lend mortgages and act as guarantor on building society loans. Additionally, the government made £100 million available to the building societies to provide 95 percent mortgages for the purchase of older houses. Grants were provided to owners to help with the cost of repairing dilapidated housing.[92] Homeownership was also subsidised through the taxation system. Owners received tax relief on their mortgage interest, and in 1963 the income tax homeowners had previously paid on the notional rental income from their property was abolished. At a time when expenditure on council housing was being reduced, the cumulative total of these subsidies was far from negligible. It is surprising, therefore, that when Labour was returned to power in

1964, these subsidies were not reversed; rather, owner occupation was further incentivised.

A NEW CONSENSUS?

There is a myth that postwar Britain was characterised by consensus, with Labour and Conservatives broadly agreeing on the idea of a mixed-economy welfare state. This was a narrative frequently heard in the 1950s and 1960s, but from the vantage of today, one is struck by the ideological division in the postwar decades. A key point of disagreement was the distribution of property rights between the owner and the state. As part of their bold reorganization of Britain, Labour radically altered the governance of the land. Although the 1947 Town and Country Planning Act fell short of their pledge to nationalise the land, it drastically limited the rights of property owners. The act made all development subject to planning control. This meant that land with planning permission would increase in value, so Labour imposed a 100 percent tax on this increase in value, effectively nationalising development rights and gains. The act also gave local authorities the right to compulsory purchase land at 1947 use values. This new distribution of property rights was central not only to the council house building programme, described in the next chapter, but also to the thirty-two new towns that sprung up across the nation in the postwar decades.

The new towns were designed to be economically self-sufficient. Each town was initiated with a sixty-year government loan. The town's development corporation used this to purchase land and start building the houses, infrastructure and amenities necessary to sustain the community. It earnt revenue renting housing, industrial and commercial sites, and releasing plots for leasehold and freehold sale. In the longer term, substantial sums stood to be made by realising the development gain—the difference between the price initially paid for agricultural land and the value of the land now that it came with planning permission and was part of a large and vibrant town. The development corporation used this income to repay the loan and invest further in the town, returning to the community the value they created.

Much like land taxation at the beginning of the century, Labour's erosion of property rights was intolerable to the Conservatives, and when they were returned to power in the 1950s they acted quickly to abolish the development tax, albeit retaining the system of planning control. This story was to repeat itself twice more in the century. Labour's Land Commission Act of 1967 taxed development increases at 40 percent. This was quickly repealed by the Conservatives in 1971. Labour was not to be disheartened and in 1976 again

introduced a development land tax, that was repealed by Thatcher's government in 1980.

Conservatives were no more enamoured to inherit the new town experiment, but unlike taxation legislation, towns cannot simply be repealed. The
financial commitments made were enormous: By 1954, £250 million had
been spent, equivalent to 6 percent of annual government expenditure.[93]
As the decade progressed, the government began to warm to the project as
the potential future returns began to be appreciated. New towns were urged
to develop commercial and industrial sites themselves, rather than selling
the land to private developers, so that the corporations could maximise the
development gain reaped in the long term.[94] By the end of the decade, the
Conservatives had announced their own generation of new towns. They
would be outdone by Labour, who in 1965 initiated the most ambitious
tranche of towns to date. It appeared that the future of the new towns was
secure: the first generation of towns was reaching maturity; many, especially
in the Southeast, were making healthy surpluses; and both parties seemed
committed to the project. The context, however, was to rapidly change. As
will be explored in subsequent chapters, when Labour came to power in the
1970s, they inherited a dire economic situation and took the decision to make
swingeing public sector cuts. Faced with a crisis of deprivation and dereliction in the inner cities as the long-term migration of industry and populations
to the suburbs and places such as the new towns was exacerbated by the
economic conditions of the 1970s, Labour took the decision to redirect its
limited resources to the inner cities and reduce the projected growth of the
new towns. It was the Conservatives, however, who sounded the final death
knell for the experiment. For Thatcher's government, the level of state intervention and planning involved in the towns was intolerable and, prioritising
ideology over economy, they ordered the development corporations to wind
up their activities and sell off their assets. In contrast to the initial plan to care-
fully dispose of assets when the development gain could be properly realised,
in the fire sale of privatisation, the corporations' property was sold off for
considerably less than it could have realised in the long term. Moreover, the
profits were simply absorbed by central government rather than given to the
communities that created this wealth.[95]

Throughout the mid-twentieth century, the parties held quite oppos-
ing views on property rights, coming to agreement only at the end of the
century. On new towns, some consensus was found by the 1950s, when
Conservatives appreciated the economics of Labour's experiment. Consensus
on the merits of owner occupation was also found by the 1950s, not by
Conservatives adopting social democratic ideals but by Labour conceding
to the Conservative position. When Labour was returned to power in 1964,
their housing policy was quite different to the 1940s. Whereas previously

the party had limited the construction of owner-occupied housing to ensure that resources were focused on council housing, by the late 1950s they were pledging that Labour would "help people buy their own homes."[96] Once in power, the party's first housing programme declared that

> once the country has overcome its huge social problem of slumdom and obsolescence . . . the programme of subsidised council housing should decrease. The expansion of the public programme now proposed is to meet exceptional needs. . . . The expansion of building for *owner occupation on the other hand is normal*; it reflects a long-term social advance.[97]

Council housing was thereby relegated to a temporary endeavour, necessary only until owner occupation could better fulfil the nation's housing needs. To this end, Labour pledged to stimulate the "growth of owner-occupation by financial measures designed to widen its economic basis."[98]

This new housing policy was in part about electoral politics. Labour feared that the Conservative critique of their housing policy was effective. From the late 1940s, the idea of the property-owning democracy was frequently debated in Labour policy documents.[99] The issue became of greater importance as the proportion of owner-occupiers increased, reaching 43 percent in 1961, yet more aspired to own.[100] It was therefore seen as vital that Labour should craft an appeal to this section of the electorate and contest the idea that the Conservatives were the party of owner-occupiers. In 1956, Anthony Crosland warned that rising affluence had "clear political implications for the Labour Party, which would be ill advised to continue making a largely proletarian class appeal when a majority of the population is gradually attaining a middle-class standard of life."[101] He urged Labour to recognise that

> its identification in the public mind with austerity, rationing, and restrictive controls is highly damaging, and that we are in grave danger of allowing the Tories to run away with the kudos of being the Party of prosperity and high consumption. We should now proudly proclaim the fact . . . that we want to see individuals happy, and rich, and enjoying what in the past have been solely the luxuries of the upper classes; and in the process we should take a long stride forward the classless society.[102]

Such a policy of affluence was for Crosland a key part of the project to rethink socialism for the conditions of the postwar age. He believed that the combination of the reforms ushered in by the 1945 Labour government and the phenomena of economic growth had fundamentally altered the terrain on which socialists operated and rendered much of prewar leftist thought obsolete: "Traditional socialism was largely concerned with the evils of traditional capitalism, and with the need for its overthrow. But today traditional capitalism has been reformed and modified almost out of existence . . . Pre-war anti capitalism will give us very little help."[103] Crosland took aim at the left's fetishization of public ownership, accusing them of confusing the means and ends of socialism. Socialism, he maintained, was about freedom and equality, and these could be better advanced through other means rather than the blunt tool of nationalisation. Economic growth, he believed, was "a precondition of their attainment" as it would allow living standards to be equalised.[104] While the immediate objective of the party must be to alleviate remaining pockets of deprivation, in the longer term Crosland believed Labour should strive for a more equitable distribution of the spoils.

These revisionist ideas had important ramifications for housing policy. If public ownership was no longer the defining feature of contemporary socialism, nor was council housing. It might be important in the short term to address the remaining housing need but was not necessarily the long-term objective of housing policy. Crosland worried about the growing status divide between owner-occupiers and council house tenants and its implications for his vision of a classless society.[105] He did not believe homeownership was offensive to socialist principles; the issue was that it had been the preserve of the more affluent. The best way to advance equality, he believed, was to open the possibility of homeownership to ever more of the population. For Crosland, as long as it was genuinely democratic and equitably distributed, the property-owning democracy was a "socialist rather than a conservative ideal."[106]

While Wilson's government did not agree with everything that revisionists such as Crosland prescribed, housing policy moved in that direction. Although council housing was a priority in the short term, Labour incentivised home-ownership in several ways. They continued and extended the favourable tax environment for owner-occupiers. When the capital gains tax was introduced in 1965, profits from the sale of primary residences were exempt. Likewise, when interest relief for loans was abolished in 1969, mortgages were specifically excluded. Those with low incomes benefitted little from mortgage interest tax relief. To extend similar benefits to lower earners, Labour introduced option mortgages, which were subsidised by the government to allow interest rates 2 percent lower than conventional loans. Guarantees were also offered to reduce the deposit required. By diminishing both the upfront and monthly costs of homeownership, Labour hoped to open owner occupation up to more of the population. This did not come cheap. By the end of the decade, tax relief and option mortgages cost the exchequer £244 million per year, compared to the £280 million spent subsidising council house tenants.[107]

Since the 1960s, the parties have worked together to subsidise owner occupation, supporting the tremendous growth in the sector. This has stalled in the new century, and despite successive governments throwing more subsidies towards the sector, over the last twenty years the proportion of the population who own their own homes has declined, especially among younger generations. Whereas it could be argued in the mid-twentieth century, when rates of homeownership consistently increased, that such subsidies were an equalising measure, as chapter 3 explores, these arguments cannot be sustained in the twenty-first century, as a declining proportion of the population are enriched by house price inflation. If in the nineteenth century they questioned whether landowners could rightfully claim the unearned increment that derived from the communal provision of urban infrastructure, surely we should question today whether the community is entitled to a share of house price inflation. Not only have owners not laboured for this, but the sector we inherit today is the product of enormous amounts of public investment across the twentieth and twenty-first centuries.

This chapter has shown the ways in which Britain's property order was made by successive generations of parliamentarians, by force, law and subsidy. The property order is, however, never simply made. It must constantly be remade in the face of new phenomena, such as democratisation. Resistance too has made the property order mutate, whether in India, Ireland or Timworth. The next chapter traces this tradition of popular resistance forward in time to explore the ways in which it forced the state to adopt a responsibility for housing the people.

NOTES

1. This section has been very much informed by E. P. Thompson, *Customs in Common: Studies in Traditional Popular Culture* (New Press/ORIM, 2015), 140–42. See also Peter King, *Crime and Law in England, 1750–1840: Remaking Justice from the Margins* (Cambridge University Press, 2006).

2. J. R. Wordie, "The Chronology of English Enclosure, 1500–1914," *Economic History Review* 36, no. 4 (1983): 502, https://doi.org/10.2307/2597236.

3. Ellen Meiksins Wood, *The Origin of Capitalism: A Longer View* (Verso, 2002), 195, 100–101.

4. Thompson, *Customs in Common*, 140–42.

5. Thomas More, *Utopia* (Wordsworth Editions, 1997), 74.

6. Ellen Meiksins Wood, *Empire of Capital* (Verso, 2005), 81–82.

7. Andro Linklater, *Owning the Earth: The Transforming History of Land Ownership* (A&C Black, 2014), 27–28.

8. Claire Priest, "Creating an American Property Law: Alienability and Its Limits in American History," *Harvard Law Review* 120, no. 2 (2006): 385–459.

9. K-Sue Park, "Money, Mortgages, and the Conquest of America," *Law and Social Inquiry* 41, no. 4 (ed 2016): 1006–35, https://doi.org/10.1111/lsi.12222.

10. Linklater, *Owning the Earth*, 78.

11. John Locke, "Of Property," in *Locke: Political Writings*, ed. (Hackett Publishing, 2003), 274–75.

12. Locke, "Of Property," 274–85.

13. Locke, "Of Property," 278.

14. Peter King, "Legal Change, Customary Right, and Social Conflict in Late Eighteenth-Century England: The Origins of the Great Gleaning Case of 1788," *Law and History Review* 10, no. 1 (ed 1992): 23, https://doi.org/10.2307/743812. 3

15. Thompson, *Customs in Common*, 140–42.

16. E. P. Thompson, *The Making of the English Working Class* (Penguin Books, 2013), 237–38.

17. Thompson, *Customs in Common*, 175, 196.

18. Partha Chatterjee, "The Colonial State and Peasant Resistance in Bengal 1920–1947," *Past and Present*, no. 110 (1986): 81–102; Ratna Ray and Rajat Ray, "Zamindars and Jotedars: A Study of Rural Politics in Bengal," *Modern Asian Studies* 9, no. 1 (1975): 81–102.

19. Alun Howkins, "From Diggers to Dongas: The Land in English Radicalism, 1649–2000," *History Workshop Journal*, no. 54 (2002): 2.

20. Jon Lawrence, "Class and Gender in the Making of Urban Toryism, 1880–1914*," *English Historical Review* 108, no. 428 (1 July 1993): 629–52, https://doi.org/10.1093/ehr/CVIII.428.629.

21. "Mr. Chamberlain at Birmingham," *Times*, 6 January 1885.

22. "Mr. Chamberlain at Birmingham."

23. Gareth Stedman Jones, *Outcast London: A Study in the Relationship between Classes in Victorian Society* (Verso Books, 2014), 16.

24. John Stuart Mill, "The Condition of Ireland," *Morning Chronicle*, 13 October 1846, 4.

25. William Thomas Thornton, *A Plea for Peasant Proprietors: With the Outlines of a Plan for Their Establishment in Ireland* (John Murray, 1848), 175.

26. Jones, *Outcast London*, 241.

27. John Bateman, *The Acre-Ocracy of England. A List of All Owners of Three Thousand Acres and Upwards . . .* (Pickering, 1876).

28. Avner Offer, *Property and Politics 1870–1914: Landownership, Law, Ideology and Urban Development in England* (Cambridge University Press, 1981), 150.

29. John Stuart Mill, "Leslie on the Land Question," *Fortnightly Review*, 1870, 672.

30. John Stuart Mill, *Principles of Political Economy: With Some of Their Applications to Social Philosophy* (Longmans, Green, Reader, and Dyer, 1866), 198.

31. John Stuart Mill, *England and Ireland* (Longmans, Green, Reader, and Dyer, 1868), 24.

32. E. D. Steele, "J. S. Mill and the Irish Question: Reform, and the Integrity of the Empire, 1865–1870," *Historical Journal* 13, no. 3 (1970): 430.

33. John Stuart Mill, "Hansard, Vol. 183 Cc.1087," 17 May 1866.

34. Mill, *England and Ireland*, 45, 9–11.

35. *Times*, 21 February 1868, 9.

36. Land Tenure Reform Association and John Stuart Mill, *Programme of the Land Tenure Reform Association* (Longmans, Green, Reader, and Dyer, 1871), 6.

37. John Stuart Mill, "Advice to Land Reformers," in *Dissertations and Discussions* (H. Holt, 1875), 270.

38. Mill, *Principles of Political Economy*, 272.

39. Jones, *Outcast London*, 161.

40. Mill, "Advice to Land Reformers," 275.

41. Land Tenure Reform Association and Mill, *Programme of the Land Tenure Reform Association*, 10.

42. Stefan Collini, *Public Moralists: Political Thought and Intellectual Life in Britain* (Clarendon Press, 1991), 323.

43. "London, Saturday, December 14, 1867," *Times*, 14 December 1867.

44. Alexander Martin Sullivan, *New Ireland* (S. Low, Marston, Searle, and Rivington, 1877), 352.)

45. *Times*, 20 August 1868, 8.

46. "House of Commons, v. 199, Cc.340," 15 February 1870.

47. Alun Howkins, *Poor Labouring Men: Rural Radicalism in Norfolk, 1872–1923* (Routledge and Kegan Paul, 1985).

48. Howkins, "From Diggers to Dongas," 13–14.

49. Henry George, "Address by Henry George in the City Hall, Glasgow on August 20, 1890," in *Henry George's Writings on the United Kingdom* (Emerald Group Publishing, 2002), 165–79.

50. "Mr. Gladstone and London Liberals," *Times*, 30 July 1887, 12.

51. Ian Packer, *Lloyd George, Liberalism and the Land: The Land Issue and Party Politics in England, 1906–1914* (Boydell and Brewer, 2001), 55.

52. Jose Harris, *The Penguin Social History of Britain: Private Lives, Public Spirit: Britain 1870–1914* (Penguin UK, 1994), 97–103.

53. Offer, *Property and Politics 1870–1914*, 146.

54. Harris, *The Penguin Social History of Britain*, 105.

55. Lord Salisbury, "Disintegration," *Spectator*, 20 October 1883, 578–79, http://archive.spectator.co.uk/article/20th-october-1883/5/-disintegration.

56. Offer, *Property and Politics 1870–1914*, 43.

57. Henry Chaplin, "House of Commons, Vol. 302, c.457," 26 January 1886.

58. E. H. H. Green, *The Crisis of Conservatism: The Politics, Economics and Ideology of the Conservative Party, 1880–1914* (Routledge, 2005), 123–24.

59. "Lord Salisbury at Exeter," *Times*, 3 February 1892, 6.

60. Roy Douglas, *Land, People and Politics: A History of the Land Question in the United Kingdom, 1878–1952* (St. Martin's Press, 1976), 52.

61. Lewis Perry Curtis, *Coercion and Conciliation in Ireland 1880–1892* (Princeton University Press, 2015), 337.

62. Timothy W. Guinnane and Ronald I. Miller, "The Limits to Land Reform: The Land Acts in Ireland, 1870–1909," *Economic Development and Cultural Change* 45, no. 3 (1997): 596, https://doi.org/10.1086/452292.

63. "Mr Balfour in Birmingham," *Times*, 23 September 1909, 7.

64. Lawrence, "Class and Gender in the Making of Urban Toryism," 651.

65. Lawrence, "Class and Gender in the Making of Urban Toryism," 646.

66. "Mr Balfour in Birmingham," 7.

67. Noel Skelton, "Constructive Conservatism," *Spectator*, 28 April 1923, 6.

68. Noel Skelton, "Constructive Conservativism IV. Democracy Stabilised," *Spectator*, 19 May 1923, 6.

69. Noel Skelton, "Constructive Conservativism III. Problem and Principle," *Spectator*, 12 May 1923, 6.

70. Philip Williamson, *Stanley Baldwin: Conservative Leadership and National Values* (Cambridge University Press, 2007), 145, 143.

71. "Abbey Road Building Society," *Times*, 27 February 1933, 20.

72. "The National Task," *Times*, 5 December 1931, 15.

73. Alan Holmans, "Historical Statistics of Housing in Britain," Cambridge Centre for Housing and Planning Research, 22 April 2015, 333, 335, https://www.cchpr.landecon.cam.ac.uk/Research/Start-Year/2005/Other-Publications/Historical-Statistics-of-Housing-in-Britain.

74. Holmans, "Historical Statistics of Housing in Britain," 130, 143.

75. "A Conservative Address," *Listener*, 1 May 1929, 38.

76. "Mr. Baldwin Appointed Premier," *Daily Mirror*, 23 May 1923, 1.

77. Sian Nicholls, "The Construction of National Identity," in *The Conservatives and British Society, 1880–1990*, ed. Martin Francis and Ina Zweiniger-Bargielowska (University of Wales Press, 1996), 135.

78. Stanley Baldwin, 'Political Broadcasts,' *The Listener*, 30 October 1935, 35.

79. Williamson, *Stanley Baldwin*, 61–62.

80. "Socialism Would Mean Inspectors All Round Bodleian Library POSTER 1929–31," accessed 25 April 2022, https://digital.bodleian.ox.ac.uk/objects/089f199a-0bb3-4d52-a227-43100476ffaf/surfaces/84393460-0f94-4ea4-b507-f9e19a64cfa7/.

81. Anthony Eden, "Nation-Wide Property-Owning Democracy," in *Freedom and Order: Selected Speeches, 1939–1946* (Houghton Mifflin, 1948).

82. Richard Toye, "Winston Churchill's 'Crazy Broadcast': Party, Nation, and the 1945 Gestapo Speech," *Journal of British Studies* 49, no. 3 (July 2010): 655–80, https://doi.org/10.1086/652014.

83. Nigel Harris, *Competition and the Corporate Society: British Conservatives, the State and Industry 1945–1964* (Routledge, 2013), 106.

84. Harriet Jones, "'This Is Magnificent!': 300,000 Houses a Year and the Tory Revival after 1945," *Contemporary British History* 14, no. 1 (1 March 2000): 102, https://doi.org/10.1080/13619460008581574.

85. Jones, "This Is Magnificent," 101–102.

86. "Post-Mortem on Voting at the Election," *Quarterly Review* 284, no. 567 (1946): 67.

87. Jones, "This Is Magnificent," 103.

88. Winston S. Churchill, "Election Address, Cardiff, 8 February 1950," in *In the Balance* (RosettaBooks, 2014).

89. Winston Churchill, "1951 Conservative Party General Election Manifesto," accessed 25 April 2022, http://www.conservativemanifesto.com/1951/1951-conservative-manifesto.shtml.

90. Jones, "This Is Magnificent," 109.

91. Harriet Overton Jones, *The Conservative Party and the Welfare State 1942–1955*. (PhD diss., London School of Economics and Political Science [University of London], 1992), 285.

92. Stephen Merrett and Fred Gray, *Owner-Occupation in Britain* (Routledge and Kegan Paul, 1982), 30–31.

93. Carol E. Heim, "The Treasury as Developer-Capitalist? British New Town Building in the 1950s," *Journal of Economic History* 50, no. 4 (1990): 907.

94. Heim, "The Treasury as Developer-Capitalist," 907.

95. I. Turok, "Public Investment and Privatisation in the New Towns: A Financial Assessment of Bracknell," *Environment and Planning A: Economy and Space* 22, no. 10 (1 October 1990): 1323–36, https://doi.org/10.1068/a221323.

96. "1959 Labour Party Election Manifesto," accessed 26 April 2022, http://www.labour-party.org.uk/manifestos/1959/1959-labour-manifesto.shtml.

97. Ministry of Housing and Local Government, "The Housing Programme," 1965, 8, cmnd. 2838, Parliamentary Papers. Italics added for emphasis.

98. Ministry of Housing and Local Government, "The Housing Programme," 89.

99. Ben Jackson, "Revisionism Reconsidered: 'Property-Owning Democracy' and Egalitarian Strategy in Post-War Britain," *Twentieth Century British History* 16, no. 4 (1 January 2005): 422, https://doi.org/10.1093/tcbh/hwi053.

100. Department for Levelling Up, Housing and Communities, and Ministry of Housing, Communities and Local Government, "English Housing Survey Data on Tenure Trends and Cross Tenure Analysis," accessed 25 April 2022, https://www.gov.uk/government/statistical-data-sets/tenure-trends-and-cross-tenure-analysis.

101. Anthony Crosland, *The Future of Socialism* (J. Cape, 1961), 216.

102. Crosland, *The Future of Socialism*, 223.

103. Crosland, *The Future of Socialism*, 61.

104. Crosland, *The Future of Socialism*, 288.

105. Crosland, *The Future of Socialism*, 109.

106. Anthony Crosland, *The Conservative Enemy: A Programme of Radical Reform for the 1960s* (Schocken Books, 1962), 39. See also chapter on property-owning democracy in Douglas Jay, *Socialism in the New Society* (Longmans, 1962).

107. Martin Boddy, *The Building Societies* (Macmillan, 1980), 188.

Chapter 2

Housing the People

RENT STRIKES

In 1915, a group of women from Glasgow led a rent strike that catalysed a fundamental shift in the way housing was organised in Britain. Cities across the UK experienced rent strikes during the first years of war, but it is not surprising that Glasgow was the epicentre of these struggles.[1] The people of Glasgow endured some of the worst housing conditions in the country. Britain rapidly urbanised across the nineteenth century. While at the beginning of the century around a third of the population lived in cities, by 1911, nearly 80 percent did.[2] Successive waves of migration by the rural dispossessed swelled the ranks of the urban poor who crowded into the nation's slums. Despite evident demand, very little housing was built for the poor, as it was far more profitable to construct suburban villas for the middle classes. The poor were crammed into decaying city centres, where, as long as one or two families were squeezed in each room and no maintenance was carried out, a reasonable profit could be drawn by the landlord.[3]

Overcrowding was therefore endemic, and the slums lacked basic sanitation, such as sewers and running water. These issues were particularly acute in Glasgow. Between 1801 and 1911, the city's population grew from 77,385 to 784,496, as migrants who had been cleared and starved off their land in Ireland and the Highlands flocked to the city.[4] Glasgow was chronically overcrowded. In 1904, 26.1 percent of urban working-class households in the North of England and 64.8 percent in London were classed as overcrowded, but in Glasgow a staggering 96.9 percent were.[5] Most working-class households in Glasgow lived in tenements rather than self-contained houses. Each tenement consisted of sixteen to twenty small flats of just one or two rooms, arranged on four floors. Facilities such as wash houses, toilets and taps were shared between the floor or even the block. This meant that as many as forty families shared a single toilet.[6] These conditions had serious repercussions. Overcrowding and poor sanitary conditions led to a high mortality rate, particularly among infants. Of those born in Glasgow in these years, one in seven did not make their first birthday.[7]

Overcrowding was exacerbated by early policy interventions designed to tackle the blight of the slums. Although the middle classes did their best to ignore the conditions endured by the poor by retreating to the suburbs, successive waves of cholera, and the periodic riots and rebellions that sprung from the slums, underlined the threat these areas posed. The middle classes feared not just the literal contagion of disease and rebellion; rather, the slums were a site onto which broader anxieties about urban life and national health were projected. Peering into these densely packed districts, the middle classes perceived the emergence of a physically and morally degenerate race amongst the dank and squalor.[8] At a time of rapid imperial expansion, the middle-class imagination was haunted by fears that this degenerate class might infect the social body and the British Empire would succumb, like Rome before, to decay at its heart. Facing a public outcry about Britain's fetid urban centres, Parliament legislated in the name of public health to empower local authorities to clear the most offensive areas, but without any obligation to rehouse the displaced. The result was further scarcity of affordable housing and yet worse conditions as the evicted crowded into neighbouring districts. Glasgow was the site of some of the largest clearance programmes. In the aftermath of a typhus epidemic in the 1860s, more than eighty-eight acres of central Glasgow were demolished, destroying at least sixteen thousand dwellings. While this cleared land stood empty for decades, overcrowding increased in surrounding districts.[9]

As well as overcrowding, tenants also contended with crippling rents. There was growing concern at the turn of the century that the working class were spending as much as a third of their income on rent. Although this might seem affordable from the perspective of twenty-first-century Britain, where nearly three-quarters of the poorest tenants pay in excess of this, in Edwardian Britain there was widespread alarm that such exorbitant rents were driving poverty and deprivation.[10] Rents ate away at what little gains were made in wages. Between 1890 and 1904, earnings increased by around 15 percent but rents rose by 36.7 percent.[11] Although it is easy to view this as pure avarice, during this period landlords saw their profit margins eroded by higher interest rates on mortgages, rising local taxes and falling property prices.[12] Rates of return for Glasgow landlords fell from 7 percent in 1890 to 3.5 percent in 1914.[13] This disincentivised new investors and mortgage lenders, as much better rates of return could be obtained from overseas investments and government bonds.[14] The construction of houses to rent virtually ceased in the first decade of the twentieth century, further compounding the housing crisis.

Although the crisis in Glasgow was particularly acute, it was symptomatic of broader problems with the rental market in Britain in the early twentieth century. It proved incapable of responding to the challenges of urbanisation. Across Britain, tenants were handing over ever greater proportions of their income for the privilege of living in overcrowded and dilapidated housing, causing poverty, disease and death. Yet even with these conditions, landlords still struggled to extract sufficient profits from working-class tenants.

As well as being a city with particularly acute housing issues, Glasgow was also distinguished by its political culture. Successive waves of migrants from Ireland and the Highlands brought with them not only a deep antagonism towards landlordism but a rich repertoire of popular protest. Property making was central to the conquest of Ireland, and this meant that resistance to the land order was key facet of broader struggles against English colonisation. It became a particularly important issue following the agricultural depression of the 1870s, which reduced the value of Ireland's crops by a quarter. Faced with radically reduced incomes, farmers were unable to pay their rents. In 1879, one thousand were evicted; in 1880, two thousand; and in 1882, five thousand.[15] Communities across Ireland came together to resist these evictions in what has become known as the Land Wars. On the ground, a campaign of violence and intimidation was waged against landlords. The numbers prosecuted for "agrarian outrages" leapt from around 200 a year in the early 1870s to 860 in 1879.[16] This wave of resistance took more official form in the guise of the Land League. Founded in 1879, the League argued that the land had been wrongfully appropriated from the people by the English invading class, who imposed a foreign system of land tenure. In recognition of their customary rights over the land, the League demanded the 3 Fs—fair rent, fixity of tenure and the free sale of tenancies. To secure these aims, and resist rent rises and evictions, the Land League coordinated a programme of direct action. In 1880, Lord Parnell, president of the League, called on members not to pay unfair rents and to ostracise those who aided evictions: "When a man takes a farm from which another has been evicted, you must shun him on the roadside when you meet him—you must shun him in the streets of the town—you must shun him in the shop—you must shun him on the fair green and in the market place, and even in the place of worship."[17]

This tactic became known as boycotting after Captain Charles Boycott, a land agent in Lough Mask in County Mayo. In 1880, his tenants asked for a 25 percent rent reduction, but this request was refused and eviction notices served to those unable to pay. When a police contingent was sent to enact the evictions, the women of the community drove them away in a hail of mud, stones and manure. Following this act of defiance, the community socially and economically ostracised Boycott, as he complained in a letter to the *Times*:

The people collected in crowds upon my farm, and some hundred or so came up to my house and ordered off, under threats of ulterior consequences, all my farm labourers, workmen, and stablemen, commanding them never to work for me again. . . . My blacksmith has received a letter threatening him with murder if he does any more work for me, and my laundress has also been ordered to give up my washing. A little boy, twelve years of age, who carried my post-bag to and from the neighbouring town of Ballinrobe, was struck and threatened on 27th September, and ordered to desist from his work.[18]

Similar campaigns of resistance took place in communities across Ireland. Rent strikes were also organised. Following the imprisonment of the League's leaders in 1881, they issued a No Rent Manifesto, calling on tenants to pay no rent until the "government relinquishes the existing system of terrorism and restores the constitutional rights of the people." In 1886, a campaign of rent strikes targeted indebted landlords. At its height, twenty thousand tenants were involved in the campaign.[19] A sign of its effectiveness can be gauged from the response of Westminster, who in 1887 passed the Coercion Act, which allowed for juryless trials for a whole raft of new crimes, including boycotting and the organisation of conspiracies against the payment of rents.

London was not the only place to notice the Land Wars. They resonated in the Islands and Highlands of Scotland, where the property order was also understood to have been imposed by a class of alien and absent landlords. Landownership was far more concentrated in Scotland than the rest of Britain. Just 1,758 landlords owned 92.8 percent of the land.[20] Their exclusive rights of ownership were secured with the utmost brutality. The Highland Clearances ran concurrent with the period of Parliamentary Enclosures. From the 1750s, landlords evicted thousands of tenants to make way for sheep and game. Tenants found themselves crowded onto poor quality marginal land where they scratched a subsistence existence as progressively more communal grazing land was enclosed. In 1881, tenants on Skye refused to pay their rents in protest at their exclusion from communal grazing lands some seventeen years earlier. When the landlord tried to evict them, the sheriff was met with a crowd of angry women who prevented the eviction. Fifty police officers were dispatched from Glasgow as reinforcements, but they too were repelled by a stone-throwing mob. Eventually, the British sent two military gunboats to restore order. This resistance inspired further acts of defiance. In the 1880s, a wave of land protests swept through the Highlands, drawing on a repertoire of protest familiar from the Irish land wars: rent strikes, eviction resistance, boycotts and "agrarian outrages."[21]

The transmission of ideas and tactics between Ireland and the Highlands was in part due their geographic proximity and the connections forged between the communities over centuries, but Glasgow was a key site of exchange between these rebellious traditions. The Glasgow Land League was central to these networks. It was established in 1880 as a branch of the Irish Land League, but from the outset large numbers of Scots participated , particularly those of Highland descent. In the Land League, the more practical traditions learnt on the land intermingled with the radical ideas that were circulating in Glasgow, especially those of Henry George.[22] Speaking to a crowd of Glaswegians in 1884, George connected the evictions in Ireland, where "at the behest of men who had never set foot in Ireland, the military forces of the empire were being used to turn out poor people from the cabins and the land on which their fathers had lived from time immemorial"; the clearances and penury in the Highlands, where communities "have to pay rents which they cannot possibly get out of the ground"; and life in Glasgow's slums and the proliferation of "want, suffering and brutal degradation, of which every citizen of Glasgow, every Scotsman, should be ashamed."[23] For George, these evils had but one cause: private property in land. This message no doubt made sense to the people of Glasgow. Not only was the memory of displacement particularly strong for those of Irish and Highlands descent, but it resonated with the tenor of experience in Glasgow's slums, where rents rose consistently across the late nineteenth century. Those unable to pay the increased rents faced eviction. This was something that landlords in Glasgow were particularly prone to. In 1913, there were more evictions in the city than in all of England and Wales.[24] Antagonisms between landlord and tenant were therefore keenly felt in the city.

The severity of the housing crisis in Glasgow meant that it was a key issue for local activist groups. Glasgow was a centre of the nascent labour movement, both in terms of the militancy that emerged from the shipyards and factories along the Clyde and the major inroads made into municipal politics. By 1898, there were ten members of the Independent Labour Party (ILP) on the town council. Alleviating the city's abysmal housing conditions was a key priority for the ILP, and they campaigned vigorously for fair rents and local authority housing.[25] Councillor John Wheatley, for example, put together a plan to provide high-quality municipal cottages to let cheaply, subsidised by the profits from the tramways.[26] Such ideas were not confined to Glasgow, and at the turn of the century, progressive councils in cities such as London and Liverpool began to explore ways in which local authorities could provide housing for the working classes.[27] But without support and funding from central government, these schemes could be little more than small-scale experiments. Significantly more pressure needed to be exerted to force national government to act.

On the ground in Glasgow, neighbourhood tenant organisations were formed to agitate for change, and women played a prominent role in these grassroots organisations. Women also made up a large proportion of the ILP's membership, and the party enjoyed close relations with the Women's Social and Political Union, which provided women in the city opportunities to gain experience in militant direct action in the fight for suffrage.[28] Similar experiences were also gained through participation in the industrial workforce. Women were at the forefront of one of the largest strikes in prewar Glasgow at the Singer factory, when in 1911 nearly eleven thousand workers walked out following the sacking of three women.[29] In 1914, the Glasgow Women's Housing Association was formed to coordinate the activities of the range of housing organisations active in the city, bringing together a group of experienced activists that included Helen Crawford and Agnes Dollan, who were both heavily involved with women's suffrage and the ILP, and Mary Barbour, who had cut her teeth in the Women's Co-operative Guild and the Tenant Defence Association in Govan.[30] This was not a group that was going to stand idly by as the housing situation rapidly deteriorated in Glasgow following the outbreak of the First World War.

Glasgow was a centre of armament production during the First World War. Following the outbreak of hostilities, workers flooded into the city looking for employment. In 1914 alone, the population of Glasgow grew by almost twenty-four thousand, but fewer than four hundred homes were built to house the growing workforce.[31] With demand outstripping supply, rents increased by a quarter in 1914.[32] Coming on top of sustained rent rises across the previous decades, even relatively affluent sections of the working class found their budgets strained by this latest increase.[33] When landlords announced a further hike at the beginning of 1915, the Glasgow Women's Housing Association decided it was time to act and organised a rent strike. The tactics pursued were relatively simple: Women went door to door persuading tenants to pledge that they would only pay the original rent and not the increases. By autumn, twenty-five thousand households across Glasgow were on strike.[34]

As well as the rich and rebellious political culture of the city, the design of the tenements themselves helped to foster the solidarity necessary to sustain such a campaign. The lack of private space meant that daily tasks, such as washing and cleaning, were conducted in communal spaces, so the women who performed the domestic work regularly came into contact with each other.[35] Tenement design, which usually had a small single entrance, also made eviction difficult, as Crawford explained:

> One woman with a bell would sit in the close, or passage, watching while the other women in the tenement went on with their household duties. Whenever the Bailiff's officer appeared on the scene to evict a tenant, the woman in the passage immediately rang the bell, and women came from all parts of the building. Some with flour, if baking. Wet clothes, if washing. Other missiles. Usually the Bailiff made off for his life, pursued by a mob of angry women.[36]

Glasgow was not the only city in which there was rent agitation in these years; tenants in cities including Leeds, Liverpool, London and Dundee were also on rent strike in 1915.[37] The strike in Glasgow was particularly successful because the group of organised and experienced women who coordinated the campaign fully capitalised on the symbolic and material power acquired by the working classes during the war.

At demonstrations they were careful to cast themselves in the mould of respectability. The strikers donned their Sunday best; children waved Union Jacks and held signs that read "While my father is a prisoner in Germany the landlord is attacking our home" and "My father is fighting in France. We are fighting the Huns at home."[38] The campaign focused on emotive cases such as the McHugh family. Michael McHugh was in hospital in France recovering from a serious wound sustained in fighting and the two eldest sons were also in the army. His wife was alone in Glasgow with five children, two of whom were seriously ill. After the landlord raised the rent, she was unable to pay the increase on top of medical bills, and when the courts ordered the family to vacate the property, a crowd of more than three thousand gathered at the house to defend them from eviction. John Wheatley, the ILP councillor, spoke. "In the long line of cruel, crushing, insulting treatment to which the Capitalist Class have subjected the working class," he pronounced, "nothing could be found to compare with their conduct in refusing the commonest shelter to the helpless children of the forgiving souls who in this crisis have placed their lives at the nation's service."[39] He incited the crowd to action: "Michael McHugh is defending his country against foreign invasion. Shettleston must defend his family against the Huns at home."[40]

The women also made the most out of the material power they had as essential war workers. The beginning of 1915 saw what is known as the shell crisis, in which a series of wartime defeats were attributed to a shortage of weapons coming out of the factories. Glasgow was one of the major centres of production; however, its output was interrupted by a series of strikes in 1915. In the factories, a parallel campaign was taking place calling for wage increases to meet rising living costs, and in autumn 1915, the housing and industrial struggles combined. The landlords helped draw them together when they attempted to use the courts to seize the wages of rent strikers. On the day of the hearing, a crowd of fifteen thousand gathered outside the courthouse, and six major munitions factories went on strike.[41] The striking workers sent a telegram to the Prime Minister warning him that unless the government stopped further rent rises, they would call a general strike.[42] Unable to risk this disruption at a vital stage in the war, the very next day the government announced its intention to introduce rent controls, prioritising the right of workers to homes over and above the right of landlords to make profit out of their properties.

The Glasgow Rent Strike was one of the most pivotal events in the history of housing in Britain. Although rent controls were intended to last only for the duration of the conflict, in the end they were not removed until the 1980s. After the end of the war, the removal of rent controls proved tricky. The restoration of market rents would exceed the ability of the working class to pay, given the fall in real wages during the war.[43] Rent rises also risked triggering serious social unrest, which genuinely terrified the governing classes in the years following the events in Russia in 1917. Continued episodes of militant unrest in the postwar period, such as that seen in Glasgow in 1919, only added to the establishment's anxieties, especially given the demobilisation of 5 million men. As the Home Office warned, "in the event of rioting, for the first time in history the rioters will be better trained than the troops."[44] Yet as long as rent controls remained in place, it was unlikely that the private sector would start building rental properties for the working class, as controls, coupled with high building costs and interest rates in the immediate postwar period, made the endeavour unprofitable. This threatened a housing shortage of such magnitude it risked triggering social unrest. This left the state little choice but to step into the breach and build the houses needed.

The 1919 Housing and Town Planning Act provided subsidies for councils to build half a million houses over three years. Introducing the bill to cabinet, Lloyd George raised the spectre of revolution haunting Europe and the threat posed to social stability by the grave housing shortage. While the housing crisis would be costly to address, he asked, "Even if it cost a hundred million pounds, what was that compared to the stability of the state?"[45] The 1919 Housing Act passed through Parliament with surprisingly little opposition. There was widespread consensus that such an ambitious housing programme was the only way to head off the revolutionary threat. But if it was to perform this function, it was essential that the houses were built to a high quality to help persuade the people that their interests were best met under the existing order. As Mark Swenarton has argued, "The new houses built by the state— each with its own garden, surrounded by trees and hedges, and equipped internally with the amenities of a middle-class home—would provide visible proof of the irrelevance of revolution."[46]

In retrospect, the 1919 Housing and Planning Act appears to be a watershed. It was the first time the national government took responsibility for housing the people, but this was not the intention of its architects, and we need to understand the act as a temporary expedient to deal with the adjustment to the very particular conditions at the end of the war. These conditions were short lived. The fear of revolt quickly receded as the economic downturn and the growth of unemployment diminished the power of workers, and in 1921 the housing programme was brought to an abrupt end, with just 170,090 houses built of the 500,000 promised.[47] This was far from the end of council housing in Britain, and faced with a continual housing crisis across the midcentury, both Labour and Conservative governments contributed to one of the largest state housing programmes the world has seen. This has given rise to the impression of a consensus around housing policy, but closer examination of these policies reveals the very different assumptions and vision that motivated each party to build.

COMPETING VISIONS FOR COUNCIL HOUSING

Although we tend to associate council housing with the left, the first proposal for a nationally funded programme came from the Conservatives. In 1912 and 1913, Arthur Griffith-Boscawen twice tried to pass a housing bill through Parliament. Although these attempts failed, they are important as they reveal the ideas and motivations that lay behind Conservative housing policy for much of the twentieth century. Introducing the bills, Boscawen argued that the state must act to avert what he termed "the great national evil":

It is not only a question of physical health. It involves the whole question of mental and moral character. We cannot hope to bring up a great Imperial race in horrible slums, where no light and air can circulate, in insanitary surroundings, in places where children brought into the world have nothing to look at except what is squalid, horrible, and dirty.[48]

Boscawen echoed the public health justification for the limited housing policy of the nineteenth century and tapped into long-held anxieties about the degenerate city. These fears were inflamed at the turn of the century by the outcry surrounding the quality of recruits who enlisted during the Boer War. Major General John Maurice warned that the "state of things in which no more than two out of five of the population below a certain standard of life are fit to bear arms, is a national danger."[49] Such was the hysteria that in the immediate aftermath of the conflict, an enquiry was set up to investigate the physical deterioration of the urban working classes. The report reassured the anxious public that no evidence was found of hereditary degeneracy. The health issues detected in the working classes were instead attributed to the appalling conditions endured by the poorest classes in Britain's urban centres.[50] Limited action to address housing issues could therefore be justified on the grounds of national health, which the right accepted as a proper domain of state intervention. Although the concept of racial health would morph into public health, this trope lay at the heart of Conservative housing policy for much of the twentieth century. Neville Chamberlain, for example, justified the re-introduction of limited subsidies for council house building in 1923 by raisingthe spectre of the slums, and the "perpetual danger to the physical and moral health of the community" that substandard housing posed.[51]

Labour's housing policy drew on a different tradition of social reform that saw the provision of housing as a key part of the state's responsibility for the welfare of the people. John Wheatley, who we last encountered railing against landlords during the Glasgow rent strikes, was given responsibility for housing during Labour's first but brief spell in government in 1924. Wheatley's perspective on housing was very different to his Conservative predecessors. He grew up in a single room which he shared with ten other members of his family. As an ILP councillor in Glasgow, he campaigned tirelessly for high-quality and affordable housing for the poor. He was strongly critical of the reduced subsidies and standards ushered in by the 1923 Housing Act and accused the Conservatives of building the slums of the future: "Why do you propose these boxes for our people? Are they inferior people to you? Are they less useful to the community than you?"[52] In his own Housing Act of 1924, Wheatley increased the subsidy for housing by 50 percent; however, even with this increased subsidy, council rents were beyond the means of many of Britain's poorest households and therefore when Labour was returned to power in 1929, these provisions were supplemented with a programme to rehouse those languishing in Britain's worst slums. Councils were paid for every household rehoused and were empowered to offer rent rebates to ensure that council housing was within the means of the poorest. Labour's time in government was again short, and when Conservatives regained control in the early 1930s, they abolished all funding for council housing apart from the slum rehousing scheme. Justifying these cuts, the Conservative Minister Sir Hilton-Young argued that council housing exacerbated the housing crisis by disadvantaging private enterprise. Only by removing subsidies would the private sector be able to provide the houses needed. The problem of the slums was, however, a different matter: "It is a public health problem. It is not in the first line a problem of housing; it is a problem of ridding our social organism of radiating centres of depravity and disease." So while it was improper for the government to subsidise housing in general, slum clearance subsidies were justifiable "as a measure for the protection and preservation of the public health."[53]

This pattern was to repeat itself in the postwar period. Labour was swept to power in 1945 with a bold vision for housing, pledging to build "five million homes in double quick time." Aneurin Bevan was put in charge this ambitious programme. He was deeply critical of the Conservatives' approach. He believed linking council housing with slum clearance had caused "grave civic damage. . . . You have colonies of low-income people, living in houses provided by the local authorities, and you have the higher income groups living in their own colonies. This segregation of the different income groups is a wholly evil thing, from a civilised point of view."[54] Bevan believed that this approach would never solve the housing problem as it "looked upon houses as commodities to be bought and sold and not as a social service to be provided."[55] Labour therefore empowered councils to build for all classes and limited the construction of private housing to focus resources on its grand housing programme. As discussed in the last chapter, Labour failed to produce houses quickly enough and the Conservatives exploited this weakness at the 1951 election, pledging to deliver 300,000 houses a year by setting the private builder free. The irony is that they only fulfilled this pledge by building council housing, albeit to considerably lower standards than Labour.[56] With the target met in 1953 and the electorate sated, we see a return to a Conservative tradition of housing policy.

The Conservatives refocused attention on the slums. They argued the success of the house-building programme meant that the key issue now faced was not the supply of new housing but the condition of the existing stock, particularly in the private rented sector. They attributed the prevalence of bad conditions to rent controls, which prevented landlords from earning enough to keep their properties in order.[57] The focus on housing conditions therefore allowed Conservatives to make an argument against the long-despised rent controls but also helped reorient policy back to the 1930s. They argued that when so many people were still living in slum housing, it was "immoral" that councils were building for general needs. It meant that only a proportion of the housing built was used to rehouse those in the most need, while the subsidy was squandered on those who did not really need it. The housing of more affluent tenants was characterised as "unjust and wasteful" by Housing Minister Duncan Sandys: "Money for housing subsidies does not fall like manna from heaven. It has to be collected from the general body of taxpayers and ratepayers, many of whom are less well-off than the council tenants they are subsidising."[58] To inject a sense of "fairness" into policy, subsidies for general-needs building were cut in 1956, confining new council housing to those displaced by slum clearances, and the number of council homes built fell by more than 50 percent between 1953 and 1961.[59] In contrast to Labour's expansive vision of council housing as a universal social service that would house considerable swathes of the population, the Conservatives cast state housing in a residual role, providing only for needs that could not be met by the private sector.[60]

The second pillar of the Conservatives' housing policy was to try and increase the profitability of the private rented sector to encourage landlords to improve conditions. From 1957, rents were decontrolled when tenants moved. Although this was something the Conservatives had long fantasised about, it would turn into an electoral liability. Predictably, the act caused rents to rise but produced no real improvement in housing conditions. Moreover, because landlords could increase rents when properties were vacant, it incentivised landlords to forcibly evict tenants so they could raise the rents. Such unscrupulous behaviour received extensive media coverage, as the press homed in on the violent practices employed by landlord Perec Rachman, who was linked to the Profumo scandal through his former relationship with Christine Keeler. Coverage of "Rachmanism" therefore provided the tabloids an opportunity to continue their salacious coverage of the scandal. For Labour, such behaviour was indicative of the problems with private landlordism. Motivated by profit, it was not surprising that landlords raised rents and skimped on repairs. Labour argued for more fundamental reform, and for a brief moment in the 1950s advocated municipalisation, the nationalisation of the private rented sector. Labour proclaimed that "the private landlord who owns property in order to make money must be replaced by a public landlord treating housing as a social service"[61] Arguably the boldest policy proposal of the twentieth century, the policy was abandoned in 1961 as the party felt it did not resonate with the electorate. When returned to power, Labour repealed the 1957 Rent Act, replacing the rather crude rent caps of previous legislation with a system of "fair rents" determined by local rent officers. While such reforms would go a long way towards ameliorating the crisis today, they had little of the transformative power of municipalisation.

This sense of compromise was to pervade Labour's broader approach to housing in the 1960s. As discussed in the last chapter, Labour had by now accepted the position that owner occupation was "normal" and a "long-term social advance." In contrast, council housing was relegated to a "short term necessity" which would stop "once the country has overcome its huge problem of slumdom." Housing programmes in the meantime must focus on "clearing the great concentrations of slums."[62] Whereas in the 1940s Labour had presented council housing as a universal social service, by the 1960s Labour cast it as a residual tenure, there to help the poorest in society who had not the means to benefit from the various policies introduced to subsidise homeownership. By the mid-1960s, there was little to distinguish Labour's vision from that of the Conservatives, and as the sector was beset by crisis at the end of the decade, the party was ill placed to defend the bold vision that had animated previous generations of Labour politicians.

THE CRISIS OF COUNCIL HOUSING.

The first dimension of the crisis was economic. During the 1950s, Conservatives encouraged the use of sterling as a trading and reserve currency, and by the 1960s, £4.5 billion was held by a range of overseas governments, corporations and individual investors.[63] As the 1960s wore on, these markets began to fear that sterling was no longer a safe investment. They were worried both about the low levels of productivity that blighted British industry and the balance of payments deficit, as the country consistently imported more than it exported. The Labour victory in 1964 was of particular concern, as they feared the government might prioritise the welfare of the people over the well-being of the market. From 1964, Britain endured several waves of intense speculation against the pound, as investors sold their sterling reserves. The run on the pound intensified in the summer and autumn of 1967, and Labour was forced to devalue the currency. To address the balance of payments crisis, Labour embarked on a programme of austerity and slashed the housing budget, but this bitter medicine did little to address Britain's underlying economic issues, nor did it restore public confidence in Labour's economic management. The Conservatives were returned to government in 1970 but only exacerbated Britain's economic difficulties, as the next chapter details.

When Labour reassumed power in 1974, they inherited an economy heading from bad to worse, as the quadrupling of oil prices in 1973 intensified Britain's balance of payments deficit. Investors began to sell sterling once more. The pound fell precipitously against the dollar, declining from $2.20 in 1975 to just $1.56 in 1976.[64] Fearing economic collapse, in 1976 Labour turned to the International Monetary Fund (IMF) for a loan of $3.9 billion, the largest yet requested in the institution's history. The bailout came with stringent adjustment clauses, forcing Labour to announce £2.5 billion in public expenditure cuts, including a reduction of £150 million to the housing programme.[65] This was a massive blow to a sector already under considerable strain. Throughout the twentieth century, council housing was funded by local authority borrowing; by 1974, councils were £11.3 billion in debt.[66] The cost of servicing these loans doubled between 1973 and 1977 as interest rates rose.[67] The cutbacks of the late 1970s therefore had an enormous impact. Not only did the building of new council homes fall to its lowest level since the war, but the reduction in maintenance budgets and the resultant fall in the quality of the environment on many estates would make the council housing project harder to defend in subsequent decades.

The second dimension of the crisis concerned shifting public attitudes towards council housing. Criticism came from across the political spectrum. From the 1960s, as the left rediscovered the poverty that lingered despite the welfare state, popular attention focused on the plight of those who still struggled to access decent and secure housing. In 1966, the BBC broadcast *Cathy Come Home*, a film that traced the plight of a family as it journeyed through insecure housing and homelessness, powerfully revealing to the nation the human cost of the ongoing housing crisis. The newly formed campaigning organisation Shelter was determined not to squander the opportunity presented by the outrage generated by the film. It took out a full-page advert in the *Times* to announce its formation and elicit donations. In a style that would come to typify Shelter's campaigning material, the page was dominated by a photograph of children peering out from the grime and gloom of their slum housing, titled "Home Sweet Hell."[68] Across the late 1960s, Shelter worked with some of the foremost documentary photographers to bring the public face to face with contemporary poverty and poor housing. Focusing on the experiences of children amongst the dank and dereliction, Shelter's publications were a powerful indictment of the shortcomings of housing policy. By the end of the 1960s, the British were better housed than ever before. Much of Britain's worst-quality housing had been cleared. Nearly a third of the population were living in council housing that overall was built to high standards and was spacious, light and equipped with modern amenities. This represented a great improvement in living standards for many. As Olive Masterson recalled of her family's move to the Moulsecoomb estate in Brighton, "It was the start of a brighter life for my parents and us. . . . Just imagine being able to go upstairs to bed and being able to have a bath in a special room, to turn on the tap and obtain hot water. . . . The most magical thing of all was to press a switch and the electric light came on."[69] The overall improvement in the nation's standard of living was of little comfort to the millions still confined to substandard housing. Certain groups in society were far more likely to have to endure these conditions. Council allocations policies prioritised residents with longstanding connections to the area, excluding recent immigrant groups, who struggled to find accommodation in the private sector because of the racism of many landlords. They found themselves crowded in expensive and poor-quality housing.[70] Shelter estimated that in 1969, 3 million people were either homeless, overcrowded or living in accommodation that lacked basic amenities such as toilets and hot water. Despite the decades of investment and building, it appeared Britain had made little progress in tackling the slums.

As well as facing criticism that the housing programme had not achieved enough, it also came under attack for having done too much. The scale of slum clearance in these years was astonishing. Between 1955 and 1985, nearly 1.5 million houses were cleared and 3.66 million people displaced. A further million were impacted in the 1930s. Slum clearance represents the largest internal displacement in modern British history.[71] Because of the way slum clearance was organised, whole areas rather than individual houses were slated for demolition. These clearances took place in a context when Britain's urban landscape was radically reconfigured to make way for new shopping centres, office blocks, traffic systems and occasional civic buildings. Whole districts and communities were swept away in the name of progress. From the 1960s, there was a growing lament for these lost communities. The publication in 1957 of Peter Willmott and Michael Young's study *Family and Kinship in East End London* set the tone. They presented a highly selective and romanticised account of working-class life in Bethnal Green. Ignoring the many residents who looked forward to escaping to an estate and the higher standard of living promised, Wilmott and Young instead focused on the role that attachment to place and kinship networks played in sustaining respectable working-class culture.[72] The Civic Trust was formed in 1958 to fight for the conservation of areas threatened by clearances, and from the 1960s, groups on the ground began to resist the clearance of their communities.[73] While the notion of community was used to save traditional working-class districts from the bulldozer, opposite qualities were attributed to council estates. Wilmott and Young exaggerated the sense of community in the East End, but when it came to describing life in Debdem, the estate where many from Bethnal Green were decanted, they downplayed the affection tenants had for their new neighbourhood and presented life on the estate as an atomised and isolated experience.[74]

This new national mood had two immediate policy implications. First was a shift from clearance to improvement and the provision of grants and investment to rehabilitate rather than demolish dilapidated neighbourhoods. Initiated by Labour in 1968, these subsidies were increasingly directed towards owner-occupiers who in the property boom of the 1970s moved into areas of nineteenth-century working-class housing and contributed to the longer-term gentrification of these neighbourhoods.[75] As the middle classes moved into areas once slated for demolition, they eulogised the communities they would come to displace.[76]

Second, in the early 1970s, Conservatives seized on the renewed focus on the slums to further narrow the social function of council housing. They argued that a radical change in policy was required to "create the conditions for a final assault on the slums." Housing policy, they alleged, only exacerbated the problem. Controlled rents denied landlords sufficient profit to maintain their properties, creating new slums faster than they could be cleared. Expenditure was poorly targeted. Rents of affluent council tenants were subsidised by taxpayers, including many who were in worse housing conditions: "They take from people who can ill afford it to give to others who . . . have no need of help."[77] From the 1960s, the right-wing press demonised the affluent tenant. The *People* ran a long running campaign against "the Great Council House Scandal," where it agitated readers with stories of tenants with nice cars and good jobs who were occupying council housing while the poor languished in the slums.[78] To address this "unfairness," Conservatives proposed that council rents should be raised to "fair rents," based on the system of rent regulation Labour introduced for the private sector in 1965. Those unable to pay the higher rents should be given assistance and it was hoped that this would incentivise more affluent tenants to move into owner occupation, freeing up council housing for the poorest in society. Rather than building housing, the focus of future Conservative policy would be on "subsidising people, not bricks and mortar."[79]

Councils were unhappy about the imposition of "fair rents," as this eroded their historic right to set rents. Initially more than one hundred councils declared they would ignore the act. Support from the national Labour Party was not forthcoming, however, and the numbers soon dwindled. Although tenants' organisations across the country organised rent strikes, by the time the legislation was enacted, just two councils remained willing to take a stand: Bedwath in South Wales and Clay Cross in Derbyshire. Bedwath was quickly dealt with when a commissioner was appointed to take over the authority's housing duties; things would be a bit trickier in Clay Cross.[80] Clay Cross had a reputation for a humane and effective housing policy. By 1971, through both clearances and improvements, the Labour council had dealt with 95 percent of the district's slum housing. Around half the population lived in council housing, where they paid the lowest rents in the country. If a tenant got in arrears, the council chose not to evict them but to send round an officer to ensure they were receiving all the benefits they were entitled to. In 1972, Clay Cross announced their intention to buy up all remaining privately rented accommodation, declaring they regarded housing "as a social service, not as something the private sector can profit from." They refused to impose fair rents, despite the councillors being taken to court and individually fined. When the government sent in a housing commissioner to collect the higher rents, the council denied him access to basic resources, such as a desk, and redeployed rent collectors to office duties, making it impossible to collect the rents.[81]

Clay Cross was example of how a more radical Labour policy might have evolved had it followed the course set out in 1945, but the Labour government elected in 1974 demonstrated just how far the national party had retreated from this grand vision. Although it repealed fair rents, when the government published the conclusions from a two-year review of housing policy in 1977, there was little of the spirit that had animated previous generations. Instead, the tone was one of caution and restraint: "Resources will always be limited. We shall never be able to move forward on all fronts as fast as we would wish. That means that—in housing as other fields—it is important to make the most of available resources. Housing policy does not exist in a vacuum."[82] Given the economic crisis, it was essential that housing expenditure become more "selective and discerning." Councils were asked to draw up bids to tackle the most immediate housing issues in their areas and compete over an ever-diminishing pot of central government funding.[83]

Rather than the universal social service envisaged in 1945, councils were instructed to prioritise those in the greatest need. While undoubtedly motivated by compassion, the prioritisation of these groups would over time act to concentrate poverty and deprivation on estates. The policy review did not foresee a long-term role for council house building. It predicted that the slums would be cleared in the next decade and "public sector housing investment should decline in response to changing circumstances."[84] While council housing was represented as a temporary measure to deal with the legacies of the nineteenth-century slum, homeownership was extolled as "a basic and natural desire," and the party reaffirmed their commitment to the promotion of owner occupation,[85] promising to maintain all existing subsidies available to owners and "promote measures to widen still the opportunity for home ownership," including greater assistance for first-time buyers, a stable supply of mortgage funding and even support for council house sales. These measures, by enabling more people to become owners, would "help to solve housing problems which used to be faced largely by the public sector."[86] By the late 1970s, there was little to distinguish Labour's housing policy from that of the Conservatives. Both saw owner occupation as the most desirable form of tenure that should be actively promoted by the state. Council housing was imagined as limited and temporary. This, then, was the final dimension of the crisis of council housing. Once Labour gave up its bold vision and accepted the Conservatives' logic, the battle was already lost.

FROM THATCHER TO BLAIR

Margaret Thatcher is popularly understood to have effected a revolutionary change in housing policy. The 1980 Housing Act instituted the Right to Buy, while the 1988 Housing Act not only decontrolled rents but removed the security of tenure tenants had enjoyed. Although these reforms transformed the landscape of housing in Britain, they were not new policy innovations but long-term Conservative objectives. There had been attempts to decontrol rents in the 1920s, 1930s and 1950s; the only difference was that in 1988 Thatcher's government was successful in doing so permanently. Council house sales were also an existing commitment. As early as the 1930s, councils were given the power to sell housing with ministerial consent. Such consent was not forthcoming from the Labour government of the 1940s, but when the Conservatives were returned to power in the 1950s, sales were again permitted. Few households took advantage of this legislation. The slow pace of sales frustrated Conservatives, who blamed it on the recalcitrance of Labour councils and called for tenants to be given a statutory right to purchase. Given the lack of demand, this was an idea that simmered on the backburner.[87] The Labour government of the 1960s did not initial contest the right of councils to sell, largely because the number of sales was negligible and of little consequence for broader housing policy, but as a number of key urban councils, such as London and Birmingham, fell under Conservative control and enthusiastically promoted council house sales, in 1968 Labour acted to limit the number of houses that could be sold. The success of sales in cities such as Birmingham demonstrated to Conservatives that there was now a sizable demand from tenants to own their own homes, a view confirmed in the early 1970s when sales peaked at forty-six thousand a year.[88] Given that many Labour councils still disallowed sales, Conservatives recognised this as a potent political issue, and at the 1974 election they rallied against councils that prevented tenants from buying, pledging to give all tenants the right to buy their homes.[89] Although they lost this election, in the aftermath of defeat responsibility for housing was given to Thatcher, who in opposition campaigned for the right to buy.[90] At the 1979 election, the Conservatives promised to not only grant this right but give tenants far larger discounts than previously enjoyed. Whereas discounts had been capped at 20 percent, the 1980 Housing Act gave tenants a reduction of between a third and a half, depending on the years lived at the property. Introducing the act, Michael Heseltine positioned Right to Buy as an expression of the Conservatives' long-held commitment to the property-owning democracy:

> There is in this country a deeply ingrained desire for home ownership. The Government believe that this spirit should be fostered. It reflects the wishes of the people, ensures the wide spread of wealth through society, encourages a personal desire to improve and modernise one's own home, enables parents to accrue wealth for their children and stimulates the attitudes of independence and self-reliance that are the bedrock of a free society.[91]

Under this policy, 30 percent of tenants would buy their own homes by 1996. By 1997, 2.2 million properties, worth an estimated £22 billion, had been sold at considerable discount—one of the largest ever transfers of state assets.[92]

Council house sales would not have been such a problem if they had been replaced, but during the 1980s the housing budget was slashed by 43 percent. Although local authorities kept half the receipts from sales, they were not permitted to spend this on housing until their debts were cleared. By 1996, just four hundred council houses were built each year. The funding crisis meant that councils had little choice but to raise rents, further incentivising those who could to buy.[93] There were no parallel cuts to any of the subsidies for owner occupiers. By 1982, the bill for mortgage tax relief and option mortgages was £1.495 billion, compared to £896 million spent subsidising council housing.[94] When the discounts offered on council house sales are taken into account, the dramatic reorientation of housing expenditure towards owner occupation is clear. Thatcher achieved something her predecessors had long fantasised about. She radically extracted the state from the responsibilities it had assumed across the twentieth century, both as a regulator of the private rented sector and as a provider of housing. She not only halted the ambitious building programmes of the midcentury but privatised considerable swathes of the best stock, expanding owner occupation and relegating council housing to a residual function. While her predecessors had tinkered in this direction, Thatcher's government went much further. But what really distinguished the housing policy of the 1980s was that when Labour were finally returned to power in 1997, they did not revise any of these policies substantially; rather, they accepted and extended the logic of Thatcher's housing policy.

Shortly after being elected in 1997, Tony Blair gave his first speech at the Aylesbury Estate in London. The estate was one of the most ambitious of the postwar period. Designed to house ten thousand people, it was one of the largest state housing projects in Europe. Construction began in 1967, but by the time it was completed in 1977, public attitudes to inner-city estates like Aylesbury had soured. From the late 1950s, when an enhanced subsidy was introduced for tower blocks, high-rise estates dominated urban reconstruction. Although they were vaunted as brave new communities in the sky, many suffered from issues of poor construction, something not experienced by similar developments in other countries.[95] The complexity of construction meant the field was dominated by large firms such as Taylor Woodrow and Wimpey, and councils lacked expertise for effective oversight, meaning that serious construction issues were often not discovered until tenants had moved in and could be expensive to rectify. More than £2.6 million was spent on basic remedial work on the Aylesbury Estate.[96] As well as construction issues, tower blocks failed to deliver the increased density of housing predicted. The promise that building higher would allow more people to be rehoused had motivated many urban councils to build towers, but because of the open space needed around high-rise developments, they didn't deliver any higher density than low-rise developments.[97] Given that they were much more expensive to build and maintain, tower blocks began to fall out of favour from the mid-1960s, and in 1967 Labour removed the high-rise subsidy, virtually halting the development of new tower blocks. The Ronan Point Disaster of 1968 did much to crystalise public sentiments against the tower block. A gas explosion caused an entire corner of the block to collapse, killing four. The subsequent inquiry revealed the block suffered from catastrophically bad construction. This shattered public confidence in high-rise developments, but the negative sentiments that began to be aired from the late 1960s extended beyond simply questions of design and construction.

The association between slum clearance and council housing meant that from the interwar period, the stigma that was attached to the slums pursued tenants as they forged new lives on the estates.[98] As falling maintenance budgets began to take their toll in the 1970s and rates of poverty increased as unemployment took hold, the stigmatisation of estates intensified. Inner-city high-rise estates in particular were tarnished as places of danger and criminality. Such stigmatisation undoubtedly had a racial element. Migrant households, who had been excluded from council housing because of residency requirements, had by the 1970s lived in areas long enough to qualify and because of the abysmal housing conditions they endured were rehoused quickly, often in one of the new high-rise inner-city estates.[99] As Stuart Hall documented, during the 1970s there was a moral panic centred on the figure of the black mugger. This hysteria fixed itself to black neighbourhoods, both traditional black communities and the new estates to which they moved.[100] There is a constant interplay between the racist trope of black criminality and the stigmatisation of estates. Oscar Newman came to prominence for his work on New York's high-rise projects, where he argued that the design of tower blocks was leading to an epidemic of gangs and crime. In 1974, he was invited by the BBC show *Horizon* to see if there was evidence of the same phenomenon in Britain. The programme was largely filmed on the Aylesbury Estate. Newman admitted that Britain did not yet have the crime rates of the United States, but, standing in front of a group of children playing on the estate, after the camera focused in on a young black boy, he pondered, "Will these children grow up to be the criminals we seem to have so much of in America?"[101]

The dissemination of Newman's ideas in Britain was greatly aided by the publication in 1985 of Alice Coleman's *Utopia on Trial*. The book recognised the noble ambitions of the midcentury programme to liberate the people from the slums, but her study of London's high-rise estates revealed them to be an "even worse form of bondage"[102] Coleman characterised estates as dirty, dangerous places, plagued by crime, vandalism and child neglect, a depiction reminiscent of the spectre of the Victorian slum. But while social investigators in the nineteenth century had the sense to think about the wider structural issues of poverty, employment and pay, Coleman totally ignored the rising unemployment and falling maintenance budgets of the 1970s and 1980s, placing the blame solely on design: "Living in a high-rise block does not force all its inhabitants to become criminals but by creating anonymity, lack of surveillance and escape routes, it puts temptation in their way and makes probable that some of the weaker brethren will succumb."[103] Coleman's ideas found influential ears. She gained an audience with Thatcher, who was so taken by her work that she was awarded £50 million to undertake "corrective measures" on seven London estates. King Charles was also interested in her ideas and invited her to join his "kitchen cabinet." He requested a tour of the estates she described. The first estate Coleman took him to was Aylesbury.[104] The constant stigmatisation of high-rise estates made them difficult to let and sell. Despite a discount of 70 percent offered for flats, there were few takers. As sales dramatically reduced the stock of council housing elsewhere, the poor of Thatcher's Britain were increasingly concentrated on high-rise estates.

So when Blair chose Aylesbury as the location for his inaugural speech, he selected a site that was already a potent symbol of the supposed failure of the council house project. Blair harnessed its symbolic power to create an image of the broken Britain bequeathed by nearly two decades of Conservative rule: "Behind the statistics lie households where three generations have never had a job. . . . There are estates where the biggest employer is the drugs industry, where all that is left of the high hopes of the post-war planners is derelict concrete." Tory misrule had created communities of worklessness, deprivation and crime, a socially and spatially divided society. Blair pledged that Labour would "bring this new workless class back into society and into useful work"[105] Despite rhetorically defining New Labour's project against Thatcherism, Blair reproduced the image of the failed estate that underwrote Conservative housing policy. Here, then, were the new slums, supposedly populated by a threatening and dangerous underclass. Just as his Victorian predecessors who were haunted by the spectre of a degenerate class, Blair's first instinct was to clear the spaces the poor inhabited.

The Aylesbury Estate was one of the first threatened with "regeneration." The aim was to fund this by transferring the estate to a housing association. This again was a policy that Thatcher's government pursued with gusto. Motivated by the desire to relegate councils to commissioners rather than providers of housing, the policy was framed in the language of tenant choice. A simple ballot would allow tenants to escape the tyranny of council control. The problem was that tenants kept making the wrong choice, seemingly happy with their local authority landlord. Despite the unpopularity of transfers, New Labour continued this policy, and during their time in government nearly a million council houses were transferred to other providers. By 2010, almost half of local authorities had no council housing.[106] Like Conservatives before, Labour found that tenants did not always embrace this opportunity.

At Aylesbury in 2001, on a turnout of 76 percent, 73 percent voted to keep the estate under council control. Surveys showed that aside from some issues with security and maintenance, tenants were happy living on the estate. The council was dissatisfied with the choice residents made and in 2005 decided the estate was too expensive to refurbish and needed to be demolished. To make this case to both tenants and the public at large, money that had been allocated to improve the community was allegedly used to fund a negative

PR campaign, which would see the *Times* brand Aylesbury as "The Estate from Hell," while the *Daily Mail* described it as "hell's waiting room."[107] The image of Aylesbury as a problem estate was reinforced by its regular deployment as a setting for TV crime dramas such as *Spooks* and *The Bill*. Programme makers, however, found that the estate did not always live up to its popular image. When Channel 4 came to film an ident, they found the estate did not have the gritty look they hankered for and in postproduction added rubbish, shopping trolleys, graffiti and tatty washing lines to achieve that authentic estate aesthetic. Residents objected to this constant stigmatisation of their estate and recognised the role that such images played in garnering support for its demolition.As one tenant commented, "All this banter about it being full of gunned and knife yielding gangs is all just fantasy and plays right into the hands of the council. . . . as I said, this discourse, this system of statements, behind which is some kind of clear agenda."[108] One of the tenant and leaseholder organisations that led the resistance against regeneration asserted,

> Our lived experience of crime on the Estate does not match the myth—and this is borne out by the statistics. We need to counter these pernicious negative stereotypes. By listing and emphasising the many positive features of our homes that we now enjoy, and celebrating our diverse community, we strengthen our bargaining position. We are not going to be bullied into giving up good sound insulation, light, views and space.[109]

As part of their broader campaign against regeneration, residents forced the council to implement strict rules to prevent the estate being used as a backdrop for negative storylines. These organisations had less success in preventing the demolition of the estate. Despite an impressive campaign that saw part of the estate squatted and a legal campaign against the compulsory purchase of leaseholders' flats, the demolition of the estate began in 2010.

Aylesbury is just one of many large council estates across the country that was demolished in this period. Between 1997 and 2019, 135,658 households were displaced in London alone.[110] The scale of these clearances has led critics to make comparisons with the slum clearances of the midcentury. While both involved the destruction of working-class areas in prime urban sites and the displacement of large numbers of people, the comparison can take us only so far. There is a marked difference in the quality of housing stock being demolished. Although the designation of whole areas as slums meant that some houses in decent condition were included, for the most part the cleared houses lacked basic amenities such as hot water, electricity, baths or indoor toilets. They were in a poor state of repair and often overcrowded. Many tenants couldn't wait to escape and marvelled at the improved standard of living on the estate.[111] The same cannot be said about the clearances of council estates today. They are not slums. While there are exceptions, council houses were built to high standards. Although they suffered from decades of poor maintenance and disinvestment, their defects can be remedied, and renovation is a much more environmentally friendly option. In the midcentury, tenants were offered secure and high-quality council housing; no such assurances are offered to those displaced today, after sales, transfers and clearances have decimated provision. Those unable to secure council housing find themselves in the private rented sector, subject to the high rents, precarious tenancies and poor conditions that characterise the tenure. Leaseholders who bought their homes under right to buy do not fare any better. The compensation offered by the council was far less that the cost of comparative properties nearby, leaving them little choice but to leave the borough or move into the private rented sector.[112] It was the fate of leaseholders that particularly worried the planning inspector at the public enquiry into the use of compulsory purchase orders on the Aylesbury Estate. Given the high proportion of black and ethnic minority homeowners on the estate, the clearances would have a disproportionate impact on these groups, and the Secretary of State ruled that the council had not fulfilled its equalities duties.[113] The midcentury clearances were tied to a process of council house building, but this is far from the case today. The estates are being cleared to make way for luxury apartments and a smattering of (un)affordable housing. At Aylesbury, there will be nearly 800 fewer socially rented homes, while at nearby Heygate, no socially rented houses were built to replace the 1200 council houses demolished, just 82 "affordable" homes priced at 80 percent of local rents and in excess of housing benefit levels.[114] Nor was council housing built elsewhere. During the 1950s and 1960s, well in excess of 100,000 council houses were built each year; during its thirteen years in power, New Labour built just 7,870 in total.[115] It appears that we have returned once again to the very earliest response of Victorian policymakers who thought they could solve the problem of poverty by demolishing the streets and houses in which it resides.

We have forgotten many of the lessons of the past when it comes to housing. Council house building and rent control and regulation were a response to the conditions created by urbanisation and industrialisation, under which the private sector was unable to provide the people with decent housing at a price they could afford, or rather, the wage that employers were willing to pay. The poor were crowded into poorly maintained housing, creating areas of acute deprivation in Britain's urban centres. Onto these much-maligned spaces were projected a range of social fears, from disease and criminality to racial degeneracy. The abject conditions in which much of the working class resided, and the centrality of these struggles to everyday experience, fuelled generations of discontent, grievances that were successfully mobilized by the women of Glasgow in 1915. The council house programme was the most significant material gain secured by the people in modern Britain. Across the twentieth century, nearly 6 million council houses were built.[116] While there were, of course, exceptions and the stock has suffered from decades of disinvestment, they were built to high standards and represented an enormous improvement on the privately rented housing people previously resided in. Although much has now been privatised, the houses that were built by local authorities across the twentieth century form the backbone of Britain's better-quality housing stock today, enjoying standards of space and light rarely seen in contemporary developments. The vision of housing as a universal social service akin to health was disappointingly fleeting, and for understandable reasons as the housing programme matured, it   increasingly focused on rehousing those living in the worst conditions. But this acted to simply spatially relocate poverty, albeit housed in much better conditions. The old slums were never fully conquered: at the end of the 1970s, more than a million households still lived in unfit conditions. But despite the many shortcomings of the programme, in this moment, the people of Britain were better housed than they ever had been—or would be.

The catalyst for this housing programme was the situation engendered by the women of Glasgow who forced the government to introduce rent controls. But the impact of the rent strikes goes beyond council housing. One of its more surprising legacies was the role it played in stimulating the boom in owner occupation across the twentieth century. Rent controls incentivised landlords to sell their houses and seek better investments elsewhere. Between 1914 and 1975, more than 3.5 million rented houses were sold into owner occupation; before 1938, a third of these purchases were made by sitting tenants.[117] Much of the money that was once invested in the private rental market found its way into the building society movement, which, as the next chapter explores, financed the boom in owner occupation. It is strange, then, that those who champion owner occupation are some of the most vociferous critics of rent regulation.

NOTES

1. On wider struggles see David Englander, *Landlord and Tenant in Urban Britain, 1838–1918* (Clarendon Press, 1983).

2. Richard Rodger, *Housing in Urban Britain 1780–1914* (Cambridge University Press, 1995), 7. Figures refer to England and Wales.

3. Enid Gauldie, *Cruel Habitations: A History of Working-Class Housing, 1780–1918* (Barnes and Noble, 1974).

Housing the People   65

4. William Hamish Fraser and Irene Maver, *Glasgow: Volume II: 1830–1912* (Manchester University Press, 1996), 142.

5. Ian Gazeley, Andrew Newell, and P. Scott, "Why Was Urban Overcrowding Much More Severe in Scotland than in the Rest of the British Isles? Evidence from the First (1904) Official Household Expenditure Survey," *European Review of Economic History* 15, no. 1 (2011): 134.

6. Sean Damer, "State, Class and Housing," in *Housing, Social Policy and the State*, ed. Joseph Melling (Croom Helm, 1980), 82.

7. Peter Scott, *The Making of the Modern British Home: The Suburban Semi and Family Life between the Wars* (Oxford University Press, 2013), 28–29; R. A. Cage, "Infant Mortality and Housing: Twentieth Century Glasgow," *Scottish Economic and Social History* 14, no. 1 (1 May 1994): 77–92, https://doi.org/10.3366/sesh.1994.14.14.77.

8. Gareth Stedman Jones, *Outcast London: A Study in the Relationship between Classes in Victorian Society* (Verso Books, 2014).

9. C. M. Allan, "The Genesis of British Urban Redevelopment with Special Reference to Glasgow," *Economic History Review* 18, no. 3 (1965): 598–613, https://doi.org/10.2307/2592567.

10. Englander, *Landlord and Tenant in Urban Britain, 1838–1918*, 6; Ministry of Housing, Communities and Local Government, "English Housing Survey 2018 to 2019: Housing Costs and Affordability," accessed 25 April 2022, https://www.gov.uk/government/statistics/english-housing-survey-2018-to-2019-housing-costs-and-affordability.

11. Scott, *The Making of the Modern British Home*, 23.

12. Avner Offer, *Property and Politics 1870–1914: Landownership, Law, Ideology and Urban Development in England* (Cambridge University Press, 1981), chap. 17.

13. Joseph Melling, "Clydeside Housing and the Evolution of State Rent Control," in *Housing, Social Policy and the State*, ed. Joseph Melling (Croom Helm, 1980), 142.

14. Martin J. Daunton, *House and Home in the Victorian City: Working-Class Housing, 1580–1914* (Edward Arnold, 1983), chap. 5.

15. Roy Douglas, *Land, People and Politics: A History of the Land Question in the United Kingdom, 1878–1952* (St. Martin's Press, 1976), 21.

16. Douglas, *Land, People and Politics*, 26.

17. Josef L. Altholz, *Selected Documents in Irish History* (Routledge, 2015), 98.

18. "Letters to the Editor," *Times*, 14 October 1880, 6.

19. Douglas, *Land, People and Politics*, 18.

20. Ewen Cameron, "Setting the Heather on Fire: The Land Question in Scotland, 1850–1914," in *The Land Question in Britain, 1750–1950*, ed. M. Cragoe and P. Readman (Palgrave Macmillan UK, 2010), 110.

21. Douglas, *Land, People and Politics*.

22. Dr Andrew Newby, *Ireland, Radicalism, and the Scottish Highlands, c.1870–1912* (Edinburgh University Press, 2007).

23. Henry George, "'Scotland and Scotsmen' 18 February 1884," in *Henry George's Writings on the United Kingdom* (Emerald Group Publishing, 2002), 125–47.

24. Englander, *Landlord and Tenant in Urban Britain, 1838–1918*, 39–40.

25. Melling, "Clydeside Housing and the Evolution of State Rent Control," chap. 4.

26. John Wheatley, *Eight Pound Cottages for Glasgow Citizens* (Glasgow Labour Party, 1913).

27. John Boughton, *Municipal Dreams: The Rise and Fall of Council Housing* (Verso Books, 2018), chap. 1.

28. Neil Gray, *Rent and Its Discontents: A Century of Housing Struggle* (Rowman and Littlefield, 2018).

29. Glasgow Labour History Workshop, *The Singer Strike Clydebank, 1911* (Clydebank District Library, 1989).

30. Joseph Melling, *Rent Strikes: Peoples' Struggle for Housing in West Scotland, 1890–1916* (Polygon Books, 1983), 31–33.

31. Melling, "Clydeside Housing and the Evolution of State Rent Control," 147; Melling, *Rent Strikes*, 59.

32. Manuel Castells, *The City and the Grassroots: A Cross-Cultural Theory of Urban Social Movements* (University of California Press, 1983), 29.

33. Castells, *The City and the Grassroots*, 28.

34. Gray, *Rent and Its Discontents*, xx.

35. Melling, *Rent Strikes*, 18–19.

36. Maggie Craig, *When the Clyde Ran Red: A Social History of Red Clydeside* (Birlinn, 2018).

37. Englander, *Landlord and Tenant in Urban Britain, 1838–1918.*

38. "Rent Strikers," 685.80.209, Burrell Collection Photo Library, accessed 26 April 2022, https://www.theglasgowstory.com/image/?inum=TGSE00906&t=2.

39. David Englander, *Landlord and Tenant in Urban Britain: The Politics of Housing Reform, 1838–1924* (PhD diss., University of Warwick, 1979), 346, http://wrap.warwick.ac.uk/2821/.

40. Ian S. Wood, *John Wheatley* (Manchester University Press, 1990), 55.

41. Melling, *Rent Strikes*, 92.

42. Damer, "State, Class and Housing," 100.

43. Daunton, *House and Home in the Victorian City*, 296–97.

44. Mark Swenarton, *Homes Fit for Heroes: The Politics and Architecture of Early State Housing in Britain* (Heinemann Educational Books, 1981), 78.

45. "Cabinet Minutes. Conclusion" (3 March 1919), CAB 23/9/26, The National Archives, Kew.

46. Swenarton, *Homes Fit for Heroes*, 87.

47. Swenarton, *Homes Fit for Heroes*, 129–35; Martin J. Daunton, *Councillors and Tenants: Local Authority Housing in English Cities, 1919–1939* (Leicester University Press, 1984), 9–11.

48. "House of Commons, Housing of the Working Classes Bill," 15 March 1912, vol 35 cc1413–95, Hansard.

49. "Where to Get Men," *Contemporary Review*, January 1902.

50. "Inter-Departmental Committee on Physical Deterioration Report of the Inter-Departmental Committee on Physical Deterioration," 1904, CD. 2175, Parliamentary Papers.

51. "House of Commons Debate," 24 April 1923, vol 163 cc303–420, Hansard.

52. "House of Commons Debate," 24 April 1923, vol 163 cc.335.

53. "House of Commons Debate," 15 December 1932, vol 273 cc559, Hansard.

54. "House of Commons Debate," 17 October 1945, vol 414 cc. 1222–23, Hansard.

55. "House of Commons Debate," 16 March 1949, vol 462 c 2123, Hansard.

56. The so-called people's homes of the 1950s were 10 percent smaller than the council houses built under Labour.

57. Ministry of Housing and Local Government, "Houses the Next Step," 1953, Cmd. 8996, Parliamentary Papers.

58. "House of Commons Debate," 17 November 1955, vol 545 cc 795, Hansard.

59. Stephen Merrett, *State Housing in Britain* (Routledge and Kegan Paul, 1979), 248–50.

60. Ministry of Housing and Local Government, "Housing in England and Wales," 1961, Cmnd. 1290, Parliamentary Papers.

61. Phil Child, "Landlordism, Rent Regulation and the Labour Party in Mid-Twentieth Century Britain, 1950–64," *Twentieth Century British History* 29, no. 1 (1 March 2018): 94, https://doi.org/10.1093/tcbh/hwx036.

62. Ministry of Housing and Local Government, "The Housing Programme," 1965, Cmnd. 2838, Parliamentary Papers.

63. Scott Newton, "The Sterling Devaluation of 1967, the International Economy and Post-War Social Democracy," *English Historical Review* 125, no. 515 (1 August 2010): 912–45, https://doi.org/10.1093/ehr/ceq164.

64. Mark Harman, "The 1976 UK-IMF Crisis: The Markets, the Americans, and the IMF," *Contemporary British History* 11, no. 3 (2008): 8, accessed 26 April 2022, https://www.tandfonline.com/doi/abs/10.1080/13619469708581446.

65. Merrett, *State Housing in Britain*, 153.

66. Merrett, *State Housing in Britain*.

67. Brian Lund, *Housing Politics in the United Kingdom: Power, Planning and Protest* (Policy Press, 2016), 166.

68. "Home Sweet Hell," *Times*, 2 December 1966.

69. Ben Jones, "The Uses of Nostalgia," *Cultural and Social History* 7, no. 3 (1 September 2010): 365, https://doi.org/10.2752/147800410X12714191853346.

70. Smith, "No Welcome Home," in *Built to Last? Reflections on British Housing Policy*, ed. John Goodwin and Carol Grant (ROOF Magazine, 1997).

71. James Alfred Yelling, "The Incidence of Slum Clearance in England and Wales, 1955–85," *Urban History* 27, no. 2 (2000): 234; James Alfred Yelling, *Slums and Redevelopment: Policy and Practice in England, 1918–1945, with Particular Reference to London* (UCL Press, 1992), 109.

72. Jon Lawrence, "Inventing the Traditional Working Class: A Re-Analysis of Interview Notes from Young and Willmott's Family Kinship in East London," *Historical Journal* 59, no. 2 (June 2016): 567–93, https://doi.org/10.1017/S0018246X15000515.

73. Ray Gosling, *St Ann's* (Civic Trust, 1967).

74. Lawrence, "Inventing the Traditional Working Class."

75. Ministry of Housing and Local Government, "Old Houses into New," 1968, Cmd. 3602, Parliamentary Papers. 2

76. Ben Jones, *The Working Class in Mid-Twentieth-Century England: Community, Identity and Social Memory* (Manchester University Press, 2018), 125–26.

77. Department of Environment, "Fair Deal for Housing," 1971, Cmnd. 4728, Parliamentary Papers.

78. K. Jacobs, J. Kemeny, and T. Manzi, "Privileged or Exploited Council Tenants? The Discursive Change in Conservative Housing Policy from 1972 to 1980," *Policy and Politics* 31, no. 3 (1 July 2003): 307–20, https://doi.org/10.1332 /030557303322034965.

79. Department of Environment, "Fair Deal for Housing."

80. Peter Malpass, "The Road from Clay Cross," in *Built to Last? Reflections on British Housing Policy*, ed. John Goodwin and Carol Grant (ROOF Magazine, 1997).

81. John Boughton, "Clay Cross Council: 'Doing Our Job—and That's to Help the Working Class, the Cream of the Nation,'" *Municipal Dreams* (blog), 31 March 2015, https://municipaldreams.wordpress.com/2015/03/31/clay_cross_part_two/.

82. Department of Environment, "Housing Policy," 1977, 2, Cmnd. 6851, Parliamentary Papers.

83. Daniel Stedman Jones, *Masters of the Universe: Hayek, Friedman, and the Birth of Neoliberal Politics—Updated Edition* (Princeton University Press, 2014), 293–94.

84. Department of Environment, "Housing Policy," 44.

85. Department of Environment, "Housing Policy," 50.

86. Department of Environment, "Housing Policy," 68.

87. Aled Davies, "'Right to Buy': The Development of a Conservative Housing Policy, 1945–1980," *Contemporary British History* 27, no. 4 (1 December 2013): 421–44, https://doi.org/10.1080/13619462.2013.824660. 4

88. Colin Jones and Alan Murie, *The Right to Buy: Analysis and Evaluation of a Housing Policy* (John Wiley and Sons, 2008), 26.

89. "October 1974 Conservative Party Manifesto," accessed 26 April 2022, http://www.conservativemanifesto.com/1974/Oct/october-1974-conservative-manifesto.shtml.

90. See, for example, Margaret Thatcher, 'Written Statement on Housing,' 27 September 1974, https://www.margaretthatcher.org/document/102411.

91. "House of Commons Debate," 15 January 1980, vol. 976 c.1445, Hansard.

92. Davies, "Right to Buy," 421; Boughton, *Municipal Dreams*, 169.

93. Boughton, *Municipal Dreams*, 175.

94. Jones and Murie, *The Right to Buy*, 37.

95. Boughton, *Municipal Dreams*, 136–37.

96. John Boughton, "The Aylesbury Estate, Southwark: 'All That Is Left of the High Hopes of the Post-War Planners Is Derelict Concrete,'" *Municipal Dreams* (blog), 7 January 2014, https://municipaldreams.wordpress.com/2014/01/07/the -aylesbury-estate-southwark-where-all-that-is-left-of-the-high-hopes-of-the-post-war -planners-is-derelict-concrete/.

97. Boughton, *Municipal Dreams*, 112.

98. Ben Jones, "Slum Clearance, Privatization and Residualization: The Practices and Politics of Council Housing in Mid-Twentieth-Century England,"

Twentieth Century British History 21, no. 4 (2010): 510–39, https://doi.org/10.1093/tcbh/hwq025.

99. Boughton, *Municipal Dreams*, 167.

100. Stuart Hall et al., *Policing the Crisis: Mugging, the State, and Law and Order* (Macmillan Education UK, 1978).

101. *Defensible Space by Oscar Newman* (Horizon, BBC, 1974), https://www.youtube.com/watch?v=9OMH7N_6nCE.

102. Alice Coleman, *Utopia on Trial: Vision and Reality in Planned Housing* (H. Shipman, 1985), 180.

103. Coleman, *Utopia on Trial*, 22.

104. Jane M. Jacobs and Loretta Lees, "Defensible Space on the Move: Revisiting the Urban Geography of Alice Coleman," *International Journal of Urban and Regional Research* 37, no. 5 (2013): 1559–83, https://doi.org/10.1111/1468-2427.12047.

105. "Blair's Speech: Single Mothers Won't Be Forced to Take Work," BBC Politics 97, accessed 26 April 2022, https://www.bbc.co.uk/news/special/politics97/news/06/0602/blair.shtml.

106. Lund, *Housing Politics in the United Kingdom*, 195.

107. Loretta Lees, "The Urban Injustices of New Labour's 'New Urban Renewal': The Case of the Aylesbury Estate in London," *Antipode* 46, no. 4 (2014): 921–47, https://doi.org/10.1111/anti.12020.

108. Lees, "The Urban Injustices of New Labour's 'New Urban Renewal,'" 929.

109. Aylesbury Tenants and Leaseholders First, "Aylesbury Area Action (Demolition) Plan," accessed 26 April 2022, http://aylesburytenantsfirst.org.uk/.

110. Loretta Lees and Hannah White, "The Social Cleansing of London Council Estates: Everyday Experiences of 'Accumulative Dispossession,'" *Housing Studies* 35, no. 10 (25 November 2020): 1701–22, https://doi.org/10.1080/02673037.2019.1680814.

111. Jones, "Slum Clearance, Privatization and Residualization"; Michael Romyn, "The Heygate: Community Life in an Inner-City Estate, 1974–2011," *History Workshop Journal* 81, no. 1 (1 April 2016): 197–230, https://doi.org/10.1093/hwj/dbw013.

112. Lees and White, "The Social Cleansing of London Council Estates."

113. Jane Rendell, "'Arry's Bar: Condensing and Displacing on the Aylesbury Estate," *Journal of Architecture* 22, no. 3 (3 April 2017): 532–54, https://doi.org/10.1080/13602365.2017.1310125.

114. Aylesbury Now, "FAQs," accessed 26 April 2022, http://www.aylesburynow.london/contact/faqs; Lees and White, "The Social Cleansing of London Council Estates."

115. Boughton, *Municipal Dreams*, 248.

116. Calculated from Alan Holmans, "Historical Statistics of Housing in Britain," Cambridge Centre for Housing and Planning Research, 22 April 2015, 47, 49, https://www.cchpr.landecon.cam.ac.uk/Research/Start-Year/2005/Other-Publications/Historical-Statistics-of-Housing-in-Britain.

117. Stephen Merrett and Fred Gray, *Owner-Occupation in Britain* (Routledge and Kegan Paul, 1982), 134–35.

Chapter 3

Boom and Bust

The Growth of Housing Finance

ELSY BORDERS VERSUS THE BUILDING SOCIETIES

In 1939, Elsy Borders, a housewife from Kent, very nearly brought down the entire British building society system. In 1934, she and her husband Jim, a taxi driver, bought a semi on the Coney Estate, one of the many privately constructed suburban estates developed in interwar Britain. The Borders were unable to view the property before purchase but were reassured by claims made in the brochure that the Bradford Third Equitable Building Society had inspected the construction of the estate and offered all purchasers 95 percent mortgages. Shortly after moving in, the property developed a series of serious structural faults: the roof leaked; the walls were damp and infested with insects; the foundations were inadequate, leading the walls to warp and windows to jam; and the electrics were faulty, causing the walls to occasionally discharge a shock. Rectifying the shoddy construction would cost more than the house was worth. The couple named the house "Insanity," making them the Borders of Insanity. This was hardly the dream of owner occupation that had been sold.

Elsy was not deterred by the fact the developer, Morrell's, had gone bankrupt and instead pursued the building society. She organized a residents' association and in 1937 persuaded five hundred households on the estate to withhold their mortgage repayments. The building society responded by taking the Borders to court for repossession, but Elsy made a counterclaim for the cost of repairs and questioned the whole legality of the society's relationship with the builder. The house was sold under a scheme known as the builders' pools. When the house was purchased, rather than paying all the money to the builder, societies withheld a proportion to act as collateral.

71

Once the buyer had paid off enough to reach a more normal loan-to-value ratio, the money was released to the builder. Builders were required in the case of default to repurchase the house for the value outstanding on the loan. This system ensured a flow of financed buyers for builders while allowing societies to lend to those without large deposits, safe in the knowledge that if the buyer defaulted they could recoup the money from the builder. The only problem was that this was not permitted under the Building Society Acts. Not only did the Borders have a legal case, they were also garnering popular support. Unable to afford legal costs, after giving herself a crash course in law at the LSE, Elsy decided to represent herself. In court, she was witty and articulate, capturing the attention of the media. The case resonated with households across the country who had invested their dreams and savings in shoddily built houses. In sympathy with the case and angered by their own housing problems, around three thousand households went out on mortgage strike. So concerned were the government that the Borders might win and invalidate all mortgages advanced in this way, a committee that included the Chancellor, the Minister for Health and the Attorney General was appointed to look into the matter. Given that 50 percent of mortgages were understood to be lent through the pools system, the Borders's case posed a grave threat to the building society movement.[1]

The growth of the societies across the interwar years and the key role they played in Conservative housing policy meant that their collapse threatened the economic health and political stability of the nation. The building societies had evolved a long way from the working-class mutual organisations, often organised around pubs, that sprung up in Britain's emerging cities in the late eighteenth century. Building society members paid into a fund that sequentially loaned money to build or buy a house. There was a tremendous growth in such societies in the nineteenth century, spurred by the political endorsement of both parties. For Liberals, they were a mechanism through which to widen the distribution of property and effect a change in the composition of parliament. They sought to create new voters by exploiting a provision that gave forty-shilling freeholders the vote in county seats. By creating freehold societies that bought up tracts of land and divided them into forty-shilling plots, societies gave the new landowners not only somewhere to build a house but also the right to vote. These schemes were very popular. In an age when interruption to employment could quickly result in eviction and in desperate cases the workhouse, property ownership conferred economic security and social and political status. By 1854, there were more than 130 societies in existence with a membership of more than eighty-five thousand.[2] It was not, however, a very effective electoral strategy. The votes created were too dispersed to significantly influence elections, and contemporaries speculated that freeholders were more likely to be Tory than Radical.[3] Indeed,

Conservatives supported mutual societies as an example of the ethos of thrift, independence and self-improvement they wished to promote. Launching the Hull Conservative Building Society in 1870, the local MP praised the movement that promoted "habits of providence, thrift, and economy, and a disposition to regard and improve the future of themselves and their families."[4] The endorsement of both parties enhanced public confidence in the mutual principal and by 1870 there were more than 2000 building societies in existence, with assets totalling nearly £20 million (around £2.5 billion in today's money).[5]

The close relationship between the societies and the state intensified across the twentieth century as they became the main mechanism through which politicians hoped to realise their promises of a property-owning democracy. As Stanley Baldwin admitted, the expansion of owner occupation in the interwar years had only been achieved by the government working "hand in hand with the building societies—or the other way round, if you like—in full sympathy and in full understanding."[6] This backing translated into several material advantages for the societies. From 1921, interest on building society savings was taxable at only a quarter of the standard rate, incentivising people to invest in the societies, and from 1923, local authorities were empowered to guarantee building society loans, enabling societies to lend to a wider proportion of the population.[7]

In their extensive advertising campaigns, building societies liked to boast of their political connections and mutual origins to convey an image of financial probity.[8] This was not substantiated by history. As the societies grew in the nineteenth century, they soon assumed a very different character to the mutual organisations they supplanted. In 1871, the Royal Commission on Building Societies noted that they had come "more and more under the direction and into the hands of the middle classes, and to secure to them its benefits." Societies were now "agencies for the investment of capital, rather than for enabling the industrious to provide dwellings for themselves."[9] The 1874 Building Societies Act aimed to reverse this trend by restricting the amount of deposits societies could accept to two-thirds of mortgage assets. Societies were forbidden from building themselves or investing in anything other than mortgages or government securities. These clauses generated great instability in the particular conditions of the late nineteenth century.

There was no shortage of deposits in these years, as during the recession, good investments were few and far between. But because the 1874 act linked deposits to lending, the influx of investments left societies competing for borrowers. Falling property prices meant that few people wanted to borrow, and this shortage led to the closure of many societies. Others diversified into riskier practices to survive. The Liberator was the largest building society and appeared the model of probity. Its founder, Jabez Balfour, was a Liberal MP and lay preacher, and the board was well stocked with politicians, clergymen and aristocrats. It boasted of its establishment connections in its extensive advertising campaign, which reassured customers of the safety of its investments.[10] The reality was somewhat different. Struggling to find sufficient borrowers, it circumvented the prohibition on building houses by setting up a web of shell companies. One company would acquire the land, then sell it on at an inflated price to another to develop, with the Liberator picking up the tab. By 1892, the majority of the society's business was conducted this way, and this left very few actual mortgages that could be called in if needed. Unfortunately, these were nervous economic times. The collapse of Baring's Bank in 1890 and the failure of the Portsea Island Society in 1891 made investors jittery and they began to recall their deposits. Between January and June 1892, £500,000 was withdrawn, and in September the Liberator announced it was limiting withdrawals. This triggered a run on other building societies, causing many smaller ones to collapse. The Bank of England was forced to issue an emergency loan of £500,000 to the Birkbeck, the second largest society, to prevent its collapse.[11] The government legislated to increase state oversight and financial transparency, drawing it into an ever-closer regulatory relationship with the societies. However, this did little to inject stability into the movement, and in 1911 the Birkbeck went bust. These events would, however, pale into insignificance when in the interwar years the building societies once again adopted risky practices to deal with a surplus of investments.

The societies grew rapidly in the interwar years. In 1920, they lent £25.1 million annually; by 1938 they were lending £137 million. Over the same period, savings invested with them increased from £63.9 million to £548.3 million.[12] The broader economic climate increased the attractiveness of building society investments. Rising real wages meant that more people were looking to deposit savings. In the past, the private rental market was a key site for small investments; however, the introduction of rent controls undermined confidence in the sector. Building societies represented an alternative, safe and straightforward investment, particularly in the aftermath of the Wall Street Crash of 1929, which underlined the risks of stock market investments. The societies offered competitive interest rates, and interest on savings was taxed at lower rates. For many different types of investors, building societies were a low-risk and tax-efficient way of saving. They offered competitive rates of return and could be redeemed at any point: an ideal haven for savings in uncertain economic times.

The influx of savings was once again a mixed blessing for societies. If they were to pay the interest promised, they needed to find new borrowers. The obvious way was to extend lending to lower-income households, but this of course came with greater risk of default. To get around this, the societies developed the builders' pools to insulate them from this risk. This was borne by the builder, who pledged to buy any houses that were repossessed and was required to leave a deposit with the society until the borrower had accumulated sufficient equity in the house. This enabled societies to considerably liberalise their terms. The cost of instalments was reduced by extending loans from twenty to twenty-five or even thirty years, and deposits were lowered to as little as 5 percent, reducing the upfront costs required. Because societies were insulated from the risk of default, they were less concerned about the actual value of the house or the ability of borrowers to afford repayments, as their losses were covered by the pool system. There was little incentive for them to stop issuing loans as builders offset the cost of the pool system by increasing house prices to cover their deposits. The pools system therefore acted to inflate house prices, and historians have speculated that at the end of the interwar period, all the conditions were in place for a housing market crash, had not war interrupted.[13] As we know from the recent subprime crisis, lenders use of financial mechanisms to insulate themselves from risk to lend to lower-income households builds great instability into the housing market, but in the interwar years a more immediate problem was posed by Elsy Borders.

The emergency committee assembled to examine the implications of the trial were unanimous. Not only could the building societies not be allowed to fail, but the builders' pools must also be allowed to continue. It was only through such a mechanism that the building societies could lend to lower-income households and help make reality the promise of a property-owning democracy. The cessation of the pools would trigger a collapse in housing finance, resulting in an immediate contraction in house building and widespread unemployment in construction, an industry believed to be central to Britain's fragile economic recovery.[14] The committee concluded that setting aside their illegality, "it is our unanimous view the Government cannot allow the 'builders' pool' system to be destroyed by a judgement of the Courts." They advised the government to act quickly and legislate to "validate for the past, and to authorise for the future."[15] By 1939 we can detect a configuration familiar today: the state actively persuading the people to take on debt to realise their dreams of homeownership; lenders using financial mechanisms to insulate themselves from risk to enable lending to lower-income households in a competitive and saturated market; the state drawn into an interdependent and symbiotic relationship with financial institutions as housing finance became increasingly central to the functioning of the national economy; and a government forced to intervene to prevent the collapse of institutions deemed too big to fail.

THE CRISIS OF THE 1970S

Although we tend to remember the 1970s as a period of economic crisis and political strife, it is forgotten that amid all this there was a brief but sharp property crisis. Had the Bank of England not stepped in to create a bailout fund of £2 to 3 billion, in the opinion of a senior banker at the time, the ramifications of the crisis "would have been worse than the Wall Street crash of 1929."[16] Despite the gravity of the situation, it disappeared from public consciousness surprisingly quickly, forgotten almost as soon as it happened. From the vantage of today, when the property sector has twice more triggered economic crises, it feels an important event to remember. The property crisis was overshadowed by the wider economic chaos of the decade. The 1970s were marked by an economic phenomenon that according to theory shouldn't have occurred: stagflation. On the one hand the economy experienced a sharp rise in inflation, which peaked at 27 percent in 1975.[17] On the other, unemployment steadily rose, crossing the 1.5 million mark in 1977, a truly unprecedented figure in the context of postwar Britain.[18] Keynesianism prescribed that when unemployment rose, governments should boost spending to stimulate economic growth, but when inflation was high they were meant to cut back spending to rein in inflation. When governments were faced with unemployment *and* inflation, they didn't know what to do. In their panicked response, they created the ideal conditions for a property boom and bust.

Britain's economic woes predated the 1970s. As discussed in the last chapter, the Labour government of the 1960s faced a balance of payments crisis. In 1967, they were forced to devalue the currency and in their final years in power sought to reduce the balance of payments deficit by embarking on a policy of austerity, cutting public expenditure, raising taxes, urging wage restraint and restricting the supply of money. Borrowing restrictions, it was hoped, would restrict personal consumption and lessen imports. Financial institutions, however, largely circumvented these measures, and personal borrowing continued to grow. The tight monetary policy had more of an impact on industry, on which hopes of an export boom were pinned.[19] These measures therefore did little to address the balance of payments deficit. Just three days before the election of 1970, figures were released that showed that the trade deficit had grown to £31 million, undermining public confidence in Labour's economic management at a critical juncture.[20] Conservatives centred their campaign on Labour's economic track record, pointing to tax increases, mounting unemployment and the rising cost of mortgages as evidence of Labour's economic failings. Although the polls predicted a Labour victory, on election day in June 1970, the Conservatives secured a comfortable majority.

On assuming power, it appeared initially that the Conservatives had few new economic ideas. Aside from reducing taxes and introducing more public-spending cuts, economic policy continued in much in the same vein as under Labour. The first major economic shift was initiated not by the government but by the Bank of England. In a 1971 Paper, *Competition and Credit Control*, the bank proposed a radically new way of controlling the amount of credit in the economy. Labour had tried to control credit by imposing absolute ceilings on lending, but the ingenuity of the financial sector rendered this largely impotent. The bank suggested that rather than lending ceilings, credit could be more effectively controlled using interest rates, the cost of borrowing and market forces to allocate credit, rather than direct government control.[21] Although formal lending restrictions were abolished, all thoughts of controlling interest rates were forgotten when Edward Heath's government decided to change tack on the economy. Restrictive policies had done little to ease Britain's economic woes. The economy remained sluggish, and in January 1972 unemployment reached the dreaded 1 million mark, the highest number since the war. A new approach was required: the dash for growth. The budget of 1972 aimed to stimulate the economy by cutting taxes, boosting public spending and holding interest rates low. The idea was that flooding the economy with cheap money would encourage investment in industry so that Britain could manufacture its way out of crisis. This isn't what happened. The measures certainly stimulated a borrowing boom, but most of this cash found its way into property rather than industry.

In retrospect, the flow of money into property isn't surprising. By the 1970s, inflation was running at more than 8.5 percent. If investors wanted to make a profit, they needed to invest in something that would provide a higher rate of return than inflation. Property was just that kind of investment. Returns from property between 1968 and 1970 were more than 10 percent higher than inflation and in the early 1970s more than 15 percent.[22] Property was therefore one of the best investments available to either institutions or individuals. Much of the money unleashed by the cheap credit boom of the early 1970s found its way into commercial property. Since the 1950s, a range of institutional investors such as insurance companies, pension funds and specialist property companies had appreciated the value of property as an inflation-beating investment. Money poured into the development of office blocks and shopping malls that radically transformed Britain's postwar city centres and sent property and land prices soaring. The unleashing of so much cheap credit in the 1970s was tinder to the flames. Bank lending to the commercial property sector rocketed from £362 million at the beginning of 1971 to £2.584 billion in 1974.[23] As early as August 1972, the Bank of England was concerned and asked the banks to reduce their lending to the property sector, but the removal of credit controls meant they had no power to enforce this, so banks kept lending.[24]

There was a concurrent boom in housing. Rising real wages across the 1950s and 1960s meant that more of the population was able to afford to buy. For those who could afford it, the range of subsidies, incentives and mortgage guarantees introduced as the political parties competed over the votes of owner-occupiers meant that owning made economic sense. There was also plenty of mortgage finance available for these eager buyers, as rising wages also meant that savings flowed into the building societies, increasing the amount available to loan. The increase in buyers and mortgage finance led house prices to creep upwards across the midcentury. In 1951, just over 300,000 people borrowed an average of £890 from the building societies; by 1970 the number of borrowers had increased to 550,000, but the average amount borrowed leapt to £3,500.[25] As in the commercial sector, the economic policies of the early 1970s intensified this phenomenon. This was in part because the relaxation of credit controls encouraged some banks to make initial forays into the residential mortgage market, increasing the amount of available housing finance. Building societies also increased their lending in these years. The low rates of interest ushered in by the dash for growth meant that building societies were able to offer much better returns on savings than the banks, and in the early 1970s the societies experienced a considerable influx of deposits, increasing the amount available to loan out.[26] But while the amount of available mortgage finance increased rapidly, houses could not be constructed that quickly. During the late 1960s, the general economic problems, the restriction of credit and the introduction of the betterment levy in 1967 produced a lull in house building. In 1970 and 1971, private completions were well below what they had been in the 1960s.[27] With the economy awash with mortgage finance but no comparative increase in houses available, prices rose sharply, doubling between 1970 and 1973.[28] This changed the mood of the builders. While in 1970 just 165,071 houses were started, 227,964 were started in 1972. By the time these houses were completed and ready to be sold, the economic climate was very different.

The property boom was brought to an abrupt halt by a sudden U-turn in policy. Given that so little credit had found its way to industry and debt-fuelled consumer spending continued apace, the dash for growth only exacerbated the balance of payment crisis. Inflation in 1973 stood at 9 percent, and following the end of the Bretton Woods's system of fixed exchange rates in 1971, the value of the pound plummeted. Without credit controls, the only mechanism the government had at their disposal was interest rates. In July 1973, the minimum lending rate was raised from 7.5 percent to 11.5 percent. This was disastrous for the commercial property sector as it was built on debt. Many property companies were already spending more than two-thirds of their profits servicing debt, leaving them massively exposed to rising interest rates.[29] Moreover, this was not conventional debt. During the development boom of the 1960s, there was a huge demand for credit, which the traditional clearing banks were unable to meet with credit controls still in place. A new shadow banking sector that operated outside the regulatory framework emerged to meet these borrowing needs. These secondary banks, as they were known, operated with a much higher degree of risk. They borrowed short term from the money markets to provide longer-term loans to property companies. As interest rates rose, their borrowing costs increased sharply. Risk also derived from the fact that the secondary banks were so confident in the property market, they were prepared to lend up to 90 percent on properties, meaning that if prices were to fall significantly, properties would no longer be worth enough to cover the loans.[30]

Events in the autumn of 1973 made a property crash highly likely. In November, in the aftermath of the oil crisis, interest rates were raised to a record 13 percent.[31] The sharp increase in the cost of borrowing dampened demand for property. More bad news was to follow in December, when the government announced a long-feared clampdown on developers' profits. Public anger had for some time been mounting at the exorbitant profits developers appeared to be making. Developers' practices hardly endeared them to the public, especially the trend in leaving newly developed property empty. Centre Point, for example, was a mixed development of offices and flats constructed in 1963 at a cost of £5.5 million; by 1973 it was valued at nearly £20 million, despite never being occupied.[32] It was deliberately left empty, as in a time of rocketing prices and rents it was more profitable to leave it vacant then get tied into long rental contracts. The sight of this prime property in central London sitting empty at a time when so many were homeless meant the building became a centre point for public anger at the development boom which had generated excessive profits for the few while radically transforming Britain's city centres and exacerbating the housing crisis. In the run-up to the 1974 election, the government attempted to placate this anger by announcing a set of tax rises for developers. This could not have come at a worse time. Property companies already struggling to pay off their debts had no reserves left to pay their taxes, leaving them with little choice but to try and sell their properties for whatever they could get, triggering the beginnings of a property crash. This was disastrous for the secondary banks. Not only were they struggling to access the short-term borrowing they depended upon to keep afloat, the value of the property they held as security was crumbling.

The first to face bankruptcy was London and County Securities Group in November 1973, followed by Cedar Holdings in December. On both occasions the Bank of England coordinated rescue operations in the hope that the crisis could be limited to just a couple of firms. This was not to be. News of the rescue deal spooked investors and within hours of the announcement of the rescue of Cedar, shares in secondary banks fell by a third.[33] The collapse of further banks posed a grave threat to the wider economy. The secondary banks were heavily indebted to the traditional clearing banks. Moreover, the clearing banks had themselves lent huge amounts to the property sector. Other key financial institutions such as pension funds and insurance companies had also invested heavily in property. If the secondary banks were not rescued, they would call in their loans, forcing indebted property owners to sell at any price, flooding the market with property that no one wanted to buy. The resultant property crash threatened to trigger a much wider crisis and spread to the financial institutions that were so dependent on property.[34] The Bank of England therefore orchestrated "the lifeboat," a fund of £2 to 3 billion to increase liquidity in the banking system, alongside agreements not to call in property debts but instead purchase property from struggling companies. Although individual property companies and secondary banks collapsed and prices fell steadily through the decade, the feared crisis was averted.

The consequences of the crash on residential housing were not as severe as in the commercial sector, nevertheless it was struck by the same pattern of boom and bust. As interest rates rose sharply across 1973, banks increased their saving rates, making building society accounts less competitive. As income from savings fell away, there was less money available to lend and fewer people able to get mortgages. As demand fell, so did house prices. This was disastrous for the house builders. During the short-lived boom, speculative builders rushed to cash in on rising house prices. This sent the cost of land soaring. Developments were planned on the assumption of continued rising prices, so falling prices were a real problem. A break was immediately applied on construction, and the number of starts fell from 216,000 in 1973 to 106,000 in 1974, a fall unprecedented in British peacetime history.[35] As dramatic as this crash was, it was also short lived, following a support package for the building societies that dwarfed the lifeboat provisions.

The problem the building societies faced was that with interest rates high, their savings rates were not competitive. Raising their own rates would entice savers back, but it would mean a corresponding increase in the mortgage rate. In 1973, the societies muted raising their rates above 10 percent, something the government was unwilling to countenance. Although Conservatives had long sought to present themselves as the party of owner-occupiers, in the early 1970s the proportion of the population who were owner-occupiers exceeded 50 percent for the first time, making mortgage rates an especially sensitive political issue. The government therefore provided a loan of £15 million to the societies on the condition that rates weren't raised for three months and requested that banks limited their rates to 9.5 percent to ease competition for savers.[36] This was not enough to stave off the pressure on the societies as the economy continued to deteriorate. Mortgage rates soon passed the 10 percent threshold, and in the spring of 1974, the building societies contemplated raising them as high as 13.5 percent. Such a move was deeply unpalatable for the new minority Labour government, and in March 1974 they provided a loan of £500 million to head off this threat—a sum considerably larger than was initially made available for the lifeboat operation.[37] In exchange for this loan, the societies agreed to work with the government to regulate the amount of mortgage finance in the economy, lending less when savings were plentiful to create a reserve for when savings fell away, with further government loans promised if necessary. In this way it was hoped that future cycles of boom and bust might be prevented.[38] In the immediate short term, pressure eased on the building societies as interest rates began to fall, restoring the competitiveness of their savings accounts. The years 1975 and 1976 saw record investment in building societies, and mortgage lending increased year on year for the remainder of the decade, enabling house prices to more than recover.[39] Demand for mortgages remained high even though rates for much of this period were above 11 percent.

There were several reasons why demand did not slacken and people were prepared to pay more than ever to own their home. First, the chances of securing a decent home in other tenures was slim. From the late 1960s, housing budgets were slashed and council house building ground to a halt. The private rented sector was smaller than ever. In a time of rent controls and rising house prices, it made economic sense to landlords to sell their properties. The range of subsidies on offer to potential owners continued to pile up: tax relief, improvement grants, mortgage schemes. By 1977, the amount of subsidies available to someone buying with a mortgage worked out, on average, more per head than for council house tenants.[40] And although rising house prices made entrance into owner occupation harder, it also made existing owners much richer. Even the more modest pace of house price inflation in the late 1970s saw the average house increase by £20 a week.[41] As the expectation of continual house prices took hold in the public imagination, so too did the belief that home ownership was a good financial investment compared to eternally shelling out rent. The crash also failed to shift attitudes of commercial property investors. In the mid-1970s, pension funds, insurance companies and banks invested record amounts in property. With prices low in the aftermath of the crash, opportunities for longer-term investment were renewed.[42] The lifeboat operation also contributed to this trend. In encouraging institutions to take property in lieu of debt, as Peter Scott highlights, the Bank of England orchestrated "an orderly transfer of assets from the property companies to the financial institutions."[43] And as the property market started to boom once again in the late 1970s, any lessons that might have been learnt about the dangers of economic dependence on property inflation were quickly forgotten.

BOOM AND BUST UNDER THATCHER AND BLAIR

Building societies had long dominated housing finance in Britain, but the programme of financial deregulation pursued by the Thatcher government enabled banks to become serious competitors. During the 1980s, they flooded the economy with mortgage finance and facilitated a far bigger housing bubble than that seen in the 1970s. The expansion of mortgage finance was not initially a conscious policy of the Conservatives. Although more than welcomed for the work it did in supporting the property-owning democracy, it was an unintentional consequence of the party's commitment to financial liberalisation.[44] Lending restrictions on banks were briefly removed in the early 1970s, but after the disastrous consequences of the dash for growth, were reintroduced in 1973. However, they were rendered ineffective by one of the Thatcher government's first acts of financial deregulation: the removal of exchange controls in 1979. This enabled banks to circumvent controls by lending through international subsidiaries. Given that controls were now impotent, they were removed in 1980, enabling banks to fully enter the domestic mortgage market. While in 1970 just 3 percent of mortgages were provided by banks, by 1982 they lent 36 percent of mortgages. Over this same period the share of building society loans fell from 88 percent to 56 percent.[45] Banks enjoyed several competitive advantages over building societies. Not only could they borrow from the wholesale money markets, but the defining feature of a bank is that the state empowers it to create new money when it makes loans. In contrast, building societies could only loan money deposited with them as savings. To level the field, building societies lobbied the government to loosen their regulatory framework, and under the 1986 Building Societies Act they were permitted to borrow money from the wholesale markets and convert to banks if their membership agreed.[46] This further increased the amount of housing finance in the economy.

The greater availability of mortgage finance without any corresponding increase in house building once again acted to inflate house prices, which increased around 10 percent each year.[47] House prices increased particularly rapidly following the announcement in the spring of 1988 that beginning in August, multiple tax relief on mortgages would be abolished. Whereas previously unmarried couples or friends buying together could each claim tax relief, in the future tax relief would be attached to the household rather than the individual. This announcement caused a rush of entrants into the housing market, eager to complete purchases before multiple tax relief was abolished.

Interest rates were also the lowest they had been for a decade, following the chancellors' attempts to stimulate the economy with cheap money in the aftermath of the stock market crash of 1987. House prices increased by nearly 30 percent in 1988.[48] The development of equity withdrawal schemes enabled homeowners to access the profits they derived from rising house prices. In combination with the explosion in various forms of unsecured debt, such as credit cards, this fuelled the consumer boom of the 1980s and marked the emergence of a new model of debt-dependent economic growth.[49]

This model began to unravel towards the end of the decade. Debt-fuelled consumption started to exert pressure on the inflation rate, which increased from 3.4 percent in 1986 to 7.8 percent in 1989.[50] Given that Thatcher was elected on a pledge to combat the high inflation that blighted the 1970s, such a rise was politically intolerable, but the government initially hesitated to increase interest rates because of the impact on mortgages and other forms of debt. When eventually the Chancellor was forced to act, he increased them several times in quick succession. Interest rates leapt from around 8 percent at the beginning of 1988 to 15 percent in 1989. This sharp rise forced lenders to increase mortgage rates. As the cost of borrowing increased, fewer people were in a position to buy, and this slackening in demand quickly translated into a fall in house prices. For those who already owned property, many found themselves unable to meet the higher cost of repayments and faced repossession. In these crisis years, one out of every hundred people who had a mortgage lost their homes.[51] As repossessed properties came on the market, often sold quickly at auction, the glut of sales accelerated the downward price cycle. Average house prices fell by a quarter between 1989 and 1992. Those who had bought at the height of the boom now found themselves with houses worth less than their mortgage debts. Among recent buyers, negative equity was very common. In 1992 in Brighton, one of the worst affected towns, 57 percent of those who had bought since 1988 were in negative equity.[52] Rising house prices had sustained the economic boom of the 1980s, but as prices began to fall this process went into reverse. Falling house prices dented consumer confidence and people stopped spending, compounding the brewing economic crisis; Britain fell into its deepest recession since the 1930s. Unemployment increased from 7 percent in 1989 to more than 10 percent in 1993.[53]

The recession of the early 1990s illustrated the dangers of debt-fuelled economic growth, however, New Labour failed to appreciate this lesson. When they were returned to power in 1997, this model of growth became the centrepiece of their economic strategy. During their period in office, Labour oversaw a house price bubble that dwarfed those of the 1970s and 1980s. Once again, the greater availability of mortgage finance without any corresponding increase in the housing stock fuelled this rise. During the 1990s and early 2000s, the construction of new houses fell to historic lows, well below other nations.[54] In 2004, Britain built 3.2 new houses per 1,000 population, compared to 19 in Ireland, 12.6 in Spain and 7.1 in America.[55] With ever more mortgage finance chasing a very slowly growing pool of houses, house prices soared. Between 1997 and 2007, the average cost of a house increased from £55,810 to £184,131, far outstripping wage growth. Over this period, the median house price increased from 3.5 to 7 times average earnings.[56]

The first factor that increased the supply of mortgage finance was the proliferation of securitisation. Mortgage-backed securities were developed in America over the course of the twentieth century by the government sponsored enterprises Fannie Mae and Freddie Mac.[57] They were first deployed in Britain in the late 1980s, but it wasn't until the 1990s that securitisation became an increasingly important facet of the UK mortgage market. Although the practice was not as extensive as in America, between 2000 and 2005, Britain accounted for 40 percent of all securitized mortgage debt in Europe.[58] To create a mortgage-backed security, lenders first set up a separate company, known as a special purpose vehicle, to sell their mortgages to. The special purpose vehicle then bundled mortgages together into bonds that could be sold and traded as a liquid asset on the international markets, supposedly priced according to risk of default. The lender derived several benefits from securitization. Rather than having to wait a long time for the mortgage to be paid back, securitization enabled lenders to realise this income quickly and draw a healthy profit from the fees charged. It was an important source of revenue for the tranche of recently demultualised building societies, which used the funds derived from securitisation to expand to compete with the larger traditional banks. Lenders also benefitted from transferring their loans to a legally separate company. Under the terms of the 1988 Basel Accords, banks were required to hold a proportion of the value of the loans they made in reserve to protect against risk of default. Securitisation allowed banks to circumvent these protections, allowing them to shift loans quickly off their balance sheets, freeing them to make new loans. Because loans were held by a legally separate company, the lender was also insulated from the risk of default. Securitisation therefore acted to increase the volume of available mortgage finance and encouraged lenders to make riskier loans.[59] In these years, we see lenders prepared to loan mortgages of ever larger multiples of income, rely on income self-certification and even provide 100 percent mortgages that required no deposit.[60] These measures, which made access to housing finance easier than ever, coincided with historically low interest rates that made it cheaper than ever to borrow. With lenders bending over backwards to provide cheap credit for homeowners, for those who could, it made sense to buy and claim their share of the windfall created by house price inflation.

The other key innovation in housing finance was the development of buy-to-let loans. A crucial prerequisite for the growth of the sector was the 1988 Housing Act, which ended rent controls and eroded tenants' security of tenure. By removing the ceiling on rents and making it easier than ever to evict tenants, the act increased the investment potential of the private rented sector. Financing the purchase of rented houses was at this point relatively expensive, as landlords were charged higher rates of interest on mortgages than owner-occupiers. In 1996, the first buy-to-let mortgages were introduced, allowing landlords to borrow on similar terms to owner-occupiers. The tax system, however, gave landlords a set of advantages over owner-occupiers. Tax relief on mortgage interest payments for owner-occupiers was progressively withdrawn across the 1990s, but as businesses, landlords could offset mortgage payments against their tax. Further benefits accrued from a tax allowance worth 10 percent of their rental income to cover wear and tear. Expenses such as insurance, letting fees and maintenance expenses were also eligible to be set against taxable income and it is estimated that by 2010–2011, landlords claimed somewhere in the region of £13 billion in tax relief.[61] Landlords also derived considerable advantage from their socioeconomic position. On average, landlords had higher incomes than the rest of the population and had already accrued significant property wealth.[62] This gave them a substantial advantage over first-time buyers, often scrabbling to save deposits as they were bled for rent in a property market that kept racing beyond their means.

Housing policy since the 1980s has acted to increase the demand for rented accommodation. House price inflation pushed owner occupation out of the reach for increasing numbers of households. The decimation of council housing meant there was little alternative to the private rented sector for those unable to buy. Although Right to Buy was intended to increase the number of owner-occupiers, in the longer term it acted to strengthen the private rented sector. By 2015, private landlords were estimated to own 40 percent of council flats sold under this policy. Some landlords even deliberately exploited Right to Buy by offering council tenants cash payments to buy their homes before selling them to the landlord to rent in the private sector.[63] The increased demand for private rented houses drove up rents, making investment in the sector an increasingly enticing prospect, especially as the low interest rates that prevailed in this period made borrowing cheaper than ever for potential landlords. Low interest rates eroded the value of returns that could be obtained from other sources of investment, such as savings and pension annuities, while the deterioration of the stock market following the bursting of the dot-com bubble at the start of the new millennium underlined the risks of shares and further eroded the performance of pension funds. Anxieties about pensions were exacerbated by a series of high-profile scandals during this period, which saw a number of schemes collapse or radically adjust their terms. The switch that many employers made in this period from final salary to defined contribution further undermined people's confidence that their pension would provide for them in later life.[64] For the middle classes anxious to protect their standard of living as they aged, housing looked like an ideal investment. Not only could an income be derived from rent, but in a time of rising house prices, large profits could be derived from this appreciation. A survey in 2004 found that for nearly 70 percent of landlords, rising house prices were central to their investment decisions.[65] These were, after all, the generations who were enriched by more than thirty years of house price inflation that gave rise to widespread expectations of continuous house price rises. In this particular conjuncture, it was not surprising that buy-to-let mortgages proved popular. At the peak in 2007, they accounted for 12 percent of the mortgage market.[66] The injection of yet more housing finance into the economy, which allowed people to buy second, third and fourth homes, significantly aggravated the house price inflation experienced in this decade.

Politicians also shared the expectation of continual house price rises. This delusion was central to New Labour's broader economic strategy, which has been described as a form of privatised Keynesianism or asset-based welfare.[67] Such paradigms were a reaction against the perceived failure of the postwar economic settlement. The model of consumer capitalism that emerged in the interwar period depended upon workers enjoying sufficient economic security that they spent and fuelled capitalist growth, and across the midcentury, workers enjoyed rising real wages. To shield the people from the instability of capitalism, the state deployed Keynesian demand management, using government debt to stimulate the economy when necessary. Further guarantees were provided by a redistributive system of welfare that collectivised the risks of what William Beveridge termed the evils of want, disease, ignorance, squalor and idleness. This paradigm came undone in the 1970s as stagflation shattered faith in Keynsianism and a political decision was taken to sacrifice the well-being of the people for the health of the economy. The abandonment of the commitment to full employment and the application of monetarism's shock cure saw unemployment rates soar, diminishing the power of labour. Thatcher's attack on the unions destroyed the more formal bargaining power that workers once enjoyed. The end of the twentieth century saw a period of stagnating wages as an ever-greater share of the pot was claimed by shareholders and management. In the context of a fragmenting welfare state, this was hardly conducive to confident consumers. How, then, could you keep the workers spending while they received an ever-decreasing share of the profits?

The answer was debt. As we have seen, economic growth in the 1980s was sustained by high levels of personal debt, whether in the form of credit cards or mortgages. But under New Labour such debt was called upon to perform a far wider social function. Instead of governments taking on debt to spend to stimulate the national economy, under privatised Keynesianism individuals were encouraged to take on debt to even out their own economic cycles. This new welfare paradigm placed responsibility on individuals rather than government to provide for themselves in times of interrupted employment, ill health and old age. The people were encouraged to save for the uncertain future by investing in assets, primarily houses, which could be drawn on in hard times. This is something that increasing numbers had to resort to. In 2003, housing equity withdrawal reached £63 billion per year, equivalent to 9 percent of all consumer spending.[68] While in the 1980s, equity withdrawals were most commonly used to fund home improvements or large items of consumption, such as cars, by 2007 this equity drawn on because of redundancy, divorce and the cost of children. Given that nearly a third of mortgage holders were taking advantage of equity withdrawal, we can see it became an everyday financial strategy for individuals and households to weather the uncertainties of life after being abandoned by the welfare state.[69] For New Labour, rising house prices were therefore a positive phenomenon. As they were excluded from the consumer price index, they did not worry the inflation target, and in 2004 the Treasury reclassified housing debt as a form of savings on the grounds that it was being used to purchase assets.[70]

New Labour sought to promote social justice by creating equal opportunities for asset ownership.[71] The 2005 election campaign centred on Labour's pledge to create a million more homeowners to make, in the words of Gordon Brown, a "home-owning, wealth owning, asset-owning democracy." Homes, he asserted, "are not just places to live" but "are becoming ever more important as assets."[72] By expanding homeownership, he would make Britain "one of the world's greatest wealth owning democracies where the widely held chance for, not just some, but all to own assets marks out a new dimension in citizenship and makes Britain a beacon for the world. Assets for all, enabling opportunity for all."[73] The expansion in homeownership would be achieved with shared ownership schemes, the extension of Right to Buy and the acceleration of housebuilding in areas of high demand in the Southeast. A rather different medicine was prescribed for areas of "low demand." Under the Housing Market Renewal Initiative, areas that had not shared in the generalised house price inflation were deemed to be failed housing markets.[74] In nine "pathfinder" areas across the North and Midlands, nearly sixty thousand houses were scheduled for compulsory purchase and demolition, not because they were structurally unsound as houses but because they performed poorly as assets. Areas were deemed cured if house prices began to rise.[75] This was the logic of New Labour's slavish devotion to rising house prices pushed to absurdity. Rather than addressing the more complex issue of Britain's regionally unbalanced economy, a new generation of slum clearance and displacement was unleashed where perfectly sound housing that would have been worth a small fortune in other parts of the country was slated for demolition simply because it had not shared in the house price inflation that afflicted the rest of the country.

THE BUBBLE THAT REFUSES TO BURST

In 2007, for the third time in little over thirty years, a property crash threatened to take down the wider economy. Its origins lay not in Britain, but the United States and the practice of securitisation. As the name implies, securities were, in theory, safe investments. They were backed by the value of the property, so if the borrower defaulted, the money could be redeemed by selling the house. In theory, by bundling mortgages together, the risk of individuals defaulting was reduced, as each individual accounted for a tiny proportion of the investor's bond. In practice, mortgage-backed securities were anything but safe. As securities diffused the risk of default away from the mortgage issuer, lenders, especially in the United States, started to provide loans to high-risk borrowers who had traditionally been denied credit. These riskier subprime loans were packaged up with other mortgages and sold on as securities, spreading the risk of default across the system. While this was meant to insulate investors from the risk of individual default, it actually meant the whole market was contaminated with very risky subprime loans. This was a major problem when borrowers began to default en masse.

House prices started to fall in the United States from 2006.[76] This was disastrous for those who had taken out subprime mortgages. When borrowers took out a subprime mortgage, they were offered a low fixed-rate mortgage for a few years, after which time their interest rates shot up. This wasn't a problem when house prices were rising, because when the teaser rates expired, the increased value of the house enabled borrowers to get a more conventional cheaper mortgage. But when house prices fell, people couldn't get new mortgages and were left trying to meet much more expensive repayments, and many fell into arrears. As they were now in negative equity, they could not repay the loan by selling their house. House prices fell further as repossessed homes flooded the market. This was an issue for lenders, who were no longer able to redeem the value of the loan through the property. It quickly became clear that mortgage-backed securities were not the safe kind of investment imagined. Borrowers in the United States had defaulted en masse and their properties were worth far less than their debts. Because loans had been bundled together in securities that had been traded across the world, no one knew exactly how the losses were distributed. All sorts of institutions, such as pension and insurance funds, now found themselves holding securities that no one wanted to buy.

With financial institutions unsure of others' exposure to these bad debts, banks became unwilling to lend to each other. As the money markets seized, institutions that had little exposure to US securities, such as Northern Rock, were drawn into the crisis. Northern Rock was one of the tranche of mutuals that converted to banks in the 1990s. Through a series of mergers, it grew to be a significant player in the UK mortgage market. It used wholesale market borrowing to fuel its expansion. By 2007, 80 percent of its funding was sourced in this way. It was dependent upon continually refinancing itself with short-term loans from the money markets to fund its loan book, meaning it was extremely vulnerable when these markets froze. When these issues were reported in the media in September 2007, a bank run began as depositors rushed to withdraw their savings from the ailing bank, compounding its liquidity problem. Although it limped on for several months thanks to Bank of England support, the steady deterioration in its financial position meant that in February 2008 it was taken into public ownership. Where Northern Rock led, others were to follow. By September 2008, several of Britain's major banks, such as HBOS and RBS, were in serious trouble and facing collapse. They were saved only by the intervention of the government, who provided a bailout fund of £500 billion.[77] Under the special liquidity scheme, banks were able to swap £287 billion worth of toxic securities for high-quality treasury bills.[78] Such extensive intervention was justified on the grounds of containing the crisis to the financial sector, as the government was concerned that if left unchecked the crisis would spread to the real economy via the contraction of mortgage lending and the resultant fall in house prices and consumer spending.[79]

This process was already underway. The financial crisis prompted a contraction in new mortgages and as the finance that fuelled the meteoric house price bubble was withdrawn, prices began to slump, falling by nearly 15 percent across 2008.[80] Ten percent of homeowners experienced negative equity, with an estimated $1.5 trillion wiped from household wealth—equivalent to 50 percent of GDP.[81] It appeared that we were going to see a repeat of the booms and busts that marked the late twentieth century. In each of the previous cycles, the ratio between house prices and earnings increased rapidly during the boom but was restored by the crash. Much to the dismay of those stuck in rented accommodation, there was no similar adjustment this time after successive governments took the decision to defend house prices, despite their professed commitment to widening owner occupation. If judged by policies and outcomes rather than rhetoric, the property-owning democracy has assumed a new character in the twenty-first century as it has sought to protect the interests of existing property owners and the money invested in houses, which in 2012 was equivalent to 61 percent of national wealth.[82]

The first and arguably most important measure that has kept house prices buoyant is the low interest rates that have prevailed since the crash. The policy response to the crisis was similar to the dash for growth in the 1970s. To try and ward off the threat of economic collapse, historically low interest rates and an enormous programme of quantitative easing flooded the economy with cheap credit. This has done very little to address Britain's productivity issues, with investment in the productive economy continuing to fall. Rather, this new dash for growth has once again acted to inflate asset prices, especially property.[83] For those able to save the necessary deposit, low interest rates have made unaffordable houses affordable when considered in terms of monthly outgoings but leaves heavily indebted buyers extremely vulnerable to interest rate rises, which in turn makes it difficult for the Bank of England to raise rates.

The low cost of borrowing has not fed through into rents. Despite landlords paying historically low mortgage rates, the cost of renting has increased since the crisis.[84] Investment has continued to flow into the buy to let market, with 80 percent of all new mortgages issued in 2015 going to wannabe landlords.[85] While lending criteria for ordinary borrowers was tightened, with substantial deposits required and interest-only loans few and far between, landlords have been able to access housing finance on more generous terms, as mortgage payments are covered by rent, which is seen to diminish lending risks. Not only has the demand for buy-to-let properties helped prevent house prices from falling, but landlords typically purchase the lower-cost housing that was once the domain of first-time buyers, making it harder than ever to get on the housing ladder. Those who would easily have been able to buy in the 1990s are stuck in rented accommodation, paying higher rents that fuel the buy-to-let market and make it harder than ever to save a deposit. Recognising the impact the sector was having on the chances of first time buyers, in 2015 the Chancellor acted to disincentivise landlords through various modifications to taxation, but the reforms were tempered to prevent a mass exodus from the sector as it was feared that this would initiate a substantial fall in house prices.[86] This in many ways typifies housing policy since the crisis, which seeks to reconcile the contradictory aims of expanding homeownership while defending the wealth already invested in the housing market.

This is exemplified by the various Help to Buy schemes. In the aftermath of a crisis that was caused by too much free and easy housing finance and the proliferation of subprime mortgages, you would think it unwise for the state to increase the amount of housing finance in the economy by enabling people to borrow more than they could afford, yet this was the essence of the Help to Buy scheme. Following the crisis there was a contraction in available mortgage finance, as lenders, having learnt lessons from the crash and wary of house price falls, imposed tougher lending criteria that required borrowers to stump up more substantial deposits. In 2013, the coalition government introduced a set of policies that would persuade lenders to release more credit into the economy, supposedly with the aim of helping first-time buyers. The first element of Help to Buy were mortgage guarantees. These aimed to restart the market in high loan-to-value mortgages by offering to guarantee 20 percent of the value of loans on house purchases up to £600,000 made by both first-time and other buyers. In the aftermath of the crisis, lenders had been reluctant to issue mortgages with small deposits, as they predicted that house prices would fall up to 20 percent and didn't want to find themselves in the position of US lenders who were repossessing houses that were now worth less than the mortgage. Under this scheme, lenders were able to recover any losses from the government if house prices fell, enabling them to restart issuing mortgages with only 5 percent deposits. The next element of Help to Buy were equity loans. Again, this was not restricted to first-time buyers; rather, all were entitled to a loan worth up to 20 percent of the value of a new-build house. By 2021, £17.4 billion had been lent in this way, enabling people who were not able to afford the prevailing high prices to purchase anyway.[87]

When the scheme was launched, critics, including the Office for Budget Responsibility, the Treasury Select Committee and the IMF, warned it was likely to inflate house prices, making it more difficult in the long run for people to become owner-occupiers. Albert Edwards, the head of global strategy at Société Générale, thought it "moronic" to solve the housing crisis by allowing a generation already burdened by student loans to get into more debt:

Why are houses too expensive in the UK? Too much debt. So what is George Osborne's solution for first-time buyers unable to afford housing? Why, arrange for a government-guaranteed scheme to burden our young people with even more debt! Why don't we call this policy by the name it really is, namely the indentured servitude of our young people.[88]

Analysis by Morgan Stanley in 2017 suggested that Help to Buy equity loans inflated the cost of new builds by 15 percent, but despite this warning the government committed another £10 billion to the scheme that year.[89] That they were seemingly unconcerned by further house price inflation is not surprising when we look beyond the rhetoric to the details of the scheme in practice. Help to Buy was not restricted to first-time buyers. The measures introduced acted to reinstate the risky lending practices that had fuelled price inflation since the 1990s and offered loans to enable people to take on debts they would not have been able to afford otherwise. By releasing the flow of mortgage finance, house price inflation resumed. But while house prices continue to climb, levels of homeownership have stagnated below what they were in the early 2000s.[90] This trend is particularly pronounced among younger generations, with rates of homeownership among those aged twenty-five to twenty-nine falling from 55 percent in 1996 to 30 percent in 2015, and from 68 percent to 46 percent for those aged thirty to thirty-four.[91] One must ask whether Help to Buy was ever intended to expand homeownership or whether its real purpose was to defend the wealth already invested in housing.

While billions have been spent defending the wealth invested in property and helping an increasingly privileged minority take the first step onto a precariously perched housing ladder, those in rented accommodation have encountered a far less beneficent state. Since the crisis, the destruction of council housing has continued apace. Punitive measures such as the 2011 Localism Act, which eroded the security of tenure traditionally enjoyed by tenants by enabling councils to offer "flexible" tenancies of as little of two years, and the Bedroom Tax, which from 2012 reduced the amount of housing benefit tenants received if they had a spare bedroom, further eroding the quality of life in the tenure. Tenants in the private sector have not fared any better. Successive governments have stood idly by as rents escalated. The only measure purportedly introduced to bring rents down was the capping of housing benefits, but this has done nothing to relieve rents; rather, it has displaced those reliant on benefits out of city centres and other high-rent areas. They have done nothing to address the abysmal conditions found all too frequently in the private rented sector, with Conservatives voting down an amendment to the Housing and Planning Bill in 2016 that would have forced landlords to ensure that their properties were fit for human habitation. Seventy-two of the 309 who voted down the amendment were themselves private landlords.[92]

The government remained blind to the fate of tenants during the COVID pandemic, offering only a stay on evictions, but fearing that the pandemic might bring about the long-anticipated house price fall, suspended stamp duty at an estimated cost of £4.7 billion.[93] This massively disadvantaged first-time buyers, who were previously exempt from the tax. The exemption sent house prices rocketing at their fastest rate in seventeen years, climbing 13.4 percent in a year: a bubble on top of a bubble on top of a bubble. Unless there is a miraculous increase in wages, this must ultimately burst, and when it does it will be those groups of people the government has "helped" to take on excessive amounts of debt that will suffer the most. Given the emotional and financial investment that existing owners have made in their homes, it is feared that a collapse in house prices will exact a heavy electoral cost. This is why time and again the Conservatives have acted against aspirant owner-occupiers to defend the wealth already invested in the housing market. This, then, is the property-owning democracy in the twenty-first century: a Parliament of property owners and landlords courting the votes of an aging and privileged clique of homeowners. Unlike the property-owning democracy of the mid-twentieth century, which oversaw an expansion of owner occupation, generationally the proportion of property owners continues to fall, and for increasing numbers it is an everyday struggle to maintain a roof over their heads. Politicians in the nineteenth century appreciated the instabilities that such a situation engenders. Joseph Chamberlain's warning remains resonant today: What ransom will property pay for the security which it enjoys?

NOTES

1. "Report of the Cabinet Committee," 25 November 1938, CAB 24/281/7, The National Archives, Kew; "Report of the Cabinet Committee," 1 February 1939, CAB 23/97/4, The National Archives, Kew.

2. E. J. Cleary, *The Building Society Movement* (Elek Books, 1965), 52.

3. F. M. L. Thomson, "Cobden, Free Trade in Land, and Road to the Abbey National," in *Rethinking Nineteenth-Century Liberalism: Richard Cobden Bicentenary Essays*, ed. Anthony Howe and Simon Morgan (Routledge, 2006), 75.

4. "Great Conservative Demonstration," *Hull Packet*, 29 April 1870.

5. Martin Pawley, *Home Ownership* (Architectural Press, 1978), 35.

6. "Abbey Road Building Society," *Times*, 27 February 1933, 20.

7. Adela Adam Nevitt, *Housing, Taxation and Subsidies: A Study of Housing in the United Kingdom* (Nelson, 1966), 53.

8. Peter Scott and Lucy Ann Newton, "Advertising, Promotion, and the Rise of a National Building Society Movement in Interwar Britain," *Business History* 54, no. 3 (1 June 2012): 399–423, https://doi.org/10.1080/00076791.2011.638489.

9. "Report of the Commissioners on Benefit Building Societies, Part I," 1872, 13–16, C. 514, Parliamentary Papers.

10. *Daily Gazette for Middlesbrough*, 1 July 1887, 1.

11. Pawley, *Home Ownership*, 44–47.

12. Martin J. Daunton, *A Property-Owning Democracy? Housing in Britain* (Faber, 1987), 104.

13. George Speight, *Building Society Behaviour and the Mortgage Lending Market in the Interwar Period: Risk-Taking by Mutual Institutions and the Interwar House-Building Boom* (PhD diss., University of Oxford, 2000), https://ethos.bl.uk/OrderDetails.do?did=1&uin=uk.bl.ethos.365489.

14. "Report of the Cabinet Committee," 25 November 1938; "Memorandum by the Chancellor of the Exchequer," 10 June 1938, CAB 24/277/22, The National Archives, Kew.

15. "Report of the Cabinet Committee," 25 November 1938.

16. Margaret Reid, *The Secondary Banking Crisis, 1973–75: Its Causes and Course* (Springer, 1982), 13.

17. Grace Blakeley, *Stolen: How to Save the World from Financialisation* (Repeater, 2019), 46.

18. Office for National Statistics, "LFS: Unemployed: UK: All: Aged 16+: 000s: SA: Annual = 4 Quarter Average," accessed 27 April 2022, https://www.ons.gov

.uk/employmentandlabourmarket/peoplenotinwork/unemployment/timeseries/mgsc/
unem.

19. Jack Copley, "Financial Deregulation and the Role of Statecraft: Lessons from
Britain's 1971 Competition and Credit Control Measures," *New Political Economy*
22, no. 6 (2 November 2017): 692–708, https://doi.org/10.1080/13563467.2017
.1311849.

20. "Trade Setback for Labour," *Times*, 16 June 1970, 1.

21. "Competition and Credit Control: Text of a Consultative Document Issued on
14th May 1971 as a Basis for Discussion with Banks and Finance Houses," *Bank of
England Quarterly Bulletin* 11, no. 2 (1 June 1971): 189–93.

22. Peter Scott, "The New Alchemy: Veblen's Theory of Crisis and the 1974 British Property and Secondary Banking Crisis," *Journal of Economic Issues* 30, no. 1 (1
March 1996): 4, https://doi.org/10.1080/00213624.1996.11505763.

23. Peter Scott, *The Property Masters: A History of the British Commercial Property Sector* (Taylor and Francis, 1996), 183.

24. Scott, *The Property Masters*, 187.

25. Pawley, *Home Ownership*, 98.

26. Stephen Merrett and Fred Gray, *Owner-Occupation in Britain* (Routledge and
Kegan Paul, 1982), 296.

27. Merrett and Gray, *Owner-Occupation in Britain*, 347.

28. Merrett and Gray, *Owner-Occupation in Britain*, 298.

29. Reid, *The Secondary Banking Crisis*, 65.

30. Reid, *The Secondary Banking Crisis*, 66.

31. Reid, *The Secondary Banking Crisis*, 81.

32. Scott, *The Property Masters*, 195.

33. Reid, *The Secondary Banking Crisis*, 11.

34. Scott, *The Property Masters*, 197.

35. Merrett and Gray, *Owner-Occupation in Britain*, 300.

36. Pawley, *Home Ownership*, 116.

37. Pawley, *Home Ownership*, 123.

38. Merrett and Gray, *Owner-Occupation in Britain*, 302–302.

39. Pawley, *Home Ownership*, 130.

40. Martin Boddy, *The Building Societies* (Macmillan, 1980), 188.

41. Pawley, *Home Ownership*, 139.

42. Doreen B. Massey and Alejandrina Catalano, *Capital and Land: Landownership by Capital in Great Britain* (E. Arnold, 1978), 128.

43. Scott, *The Property Masters*, 198.

44. Mark Stephens, "Mortgage Market Deregulation and Its Consequences,"
Housing Studies 22, no. 2 (1 March 2007): 201–20, https://doi.org/10.1080
/02673030601132797.

45. Christopher Gentle, Daniel Dorling, and James Comford, "Negative Equity and
British Housing in the 1990s: Cause and Effect," *Urban Studies* 31, no. 2 (1 March
1994): 188, https://doi.org/10.1080/00420989420080191.

46. Martin Boddy, "Financial Deregulation and UK Housing Finance: Govern-ment-building Society Relations and the Building Societies Act, 1986," *Housing Studies* 4, no. 2 (1 April 1989): 92–104, https://doi.org/10.1080/02673038908720647.

47. Apart from during the brief recession of 1981–1982. Nationwide Build-ing Society, "Annual Percentage Change in UK House Prices," accessed 27 April 2022, https://www.nationwidehousepriceindex.co.uk/resources/chart-data-download -annual-percentage-change-in-uk-house-prices.

48. Nationwide Building Society, "Annual Percentage Change in UK House Prices."

49. Engelbert Stockhammer, "Neoliberal Growth Models, Monetary Union and the Euro Crisis. A Post-Keynesian Perspective," *New Political Economy* 21, no. 4 (3 July 2016): 365–79, https://doi.org/10.1080/13563467.2016.1115826.

50. David Cobham, "The Lawson Boom: Excessive Depreciation versus Financial Liberalisation," *Financial History Review* 4, no. 1 (April 1997): 73, https://doi.org/10 .1017/S0968565000000846.

51. Danny Dorling, *All That Is Solid: How the Great Housing Disaster Defines Our Times, and What We Can Do About It* (Penguin UK, 2014), 244.

52. Gentle, Dorling, and Comford, "Negative Equity and British Housing in the 1990s," 192.

53. Office for National Statistics, "LFS: Unemployed: UK: All: Aged 16+: 000s: SA: Annual = 4 Quarter Average."

54. Alan Holmans, "Historical Statistics of Housing in Britain," Cambridge Centre for Housing and Planning Research, 22 April 2015, 50, https://www.cchpr.landecon .cam.ac.uk/Research/Start-Year/2005/Other-Publications/Historical-Statistics-of -Housing-in-Britain.

55. Brian Lund, *Housing Politics in the United Kingdom: Power, Planning and Protest* (Policy Press, 2016), 134.

56. Brian Lund, *Understanding Housing Policy* (Policy Press, 2011), 258; Nation-wide Building Society, "Annual Percentage Change in UK House Prices."

57. Kevin Fox Gotham, "Creating Liquidity out of Spatial Fixity: The Secondary Circuit of Capital and the Subprime Mortgage Crisis," *International Journal of Urban and Regional Research* 33, no. 2 (2009): 355–71, https://doi.org/10.1111/j.1468-2427 .2009.00874.x.

58. Leonard Seabrooke and H. Schwartz, *The Politics of Housing Booms and Busts* (Springer, 2009), 155.

59. T. Wainwright, "Looking to Tomorrow: The Past and Future Roles of Secu-ritisation in Residential Mortgage Funding," 2010, https://www.nottingham.ac.uk/ business/who-we-are/centres-and-institutes/gcbfi/documents/researchreports/paper80 .pdf; National Audit Office, 'Introduction to Asset-Backed Securities,' Novem-ber 2016, https://www.nao.org.uk/wp-content/uploads/2016/07/Introduction-to-asset -backed-securities.pdf.

60. Lund, *Housing Politics in the United Kingdom*, 134.

61. Lund, *Housing Politics in the United Kingdom*, 106.

62. Chris Lord, James Lloyd, and Matt Barnes, "Whose Home? Understanding Landlords and Their Effect on Public Policy," Strategic Society, 4 July 2013, https:

//strategicsociety.org.uk/whose-home-understanding-landlords-and-their-effect-on-public-policy/.

63. Lund, *Housing Politics in the United Kingdom*, 105.

64. Peter A. Kemp and Tony Crook, *Transforming Private Landlords: Housing, Markets and Public Policy* (John Wiley and Sons, 2011), 166.

65. Andrew Leyshon and Shaun French, "'We All Live in a Robbie Fowler House': The Geographies of the Buy to Let Market in the UK," *British Journal of Politics and International Relations* 11, no. 3 (1 August 2009): 446, https://doi.org/10.1111/j.1467-856X.2009.00381.x.

66. Leyshon and French, "We All Live in a Robbie Fowler House," 443.

67. Colin Crouch, "Privatised Keynesianism: An Unacknowledged Policy Regime," *British Journal of Politics and International Relations* 11, no. 3 (2009): 382–99, https://doi.org/10.1111/j.1467-856X.2009.00377.x; Matthew Watson, "House Price Keynesianism and the Contradictions of the Modern Investor Subject," *Housing Studies* 25, no. 3 (1 May 2010): 413–26, https://doi.org/10.1080/02673031003711550; Alan Finlayson, "Financialisation, Financial Literacy and Asset-Based Welfare," *British Journal of Politics and International Relations* 11, no. 3 (1 August 2009): 400–421, https://doi.org/10.1111/j.1467-856X.2009.00378.x.

68. Stuart Lowe, *The Housing Debate* (Policy Press, 2011), 192.

69. Susan J. Smith and Beverley A. Searle, *The Blackwell Companion to the Economics of Housing: The Housing Wealth of Nations* (John Wiley and Sons, 2010).

70. Peter Saunders, "Restoring a Nation of Home Owners," Civitas: Institute for the Study of Civil Society, 12 June 2016, 67, http://civitas.org.ukhttps://www.civitas.org.uk/publications/restoring-a-nation-of-home-owners/.

71. Finlayson, "Financialisation, Financial Literacy and Asset-Based Welfare."

72. *Times*, 1 April 2005, 1–2.

73. R. Ronald, *The Ideology of Home Ownership: Homeowner Societies and the Role of Housing* (Springer, 2008), 132.

74. Office of the Deputy Prime Minister, *Sustainable Communities: Homes for All* (Stationery Office, 2005).

75. Philip Leather and Brendan Nevin, "The Housing Market Renewal Programme: Origins, Outcomes and the Effectiveness of Public Policy Interventions in a Volatile Market," *Urban Studies* 50, no. 5 (1 April 2013): 856–75, https://doi.org/10.1177/0042098012449667; Anna Minton, *Ground Control: Fear and Happiness in the Twenty-First-Century City* (Penguin UK, 2012), chap. 5.

76. This section draws upon Adam Tooze, *Crashed: How a Decade of Financial Crises Changed the World* (Penguin UK, 2018).

77. Blakeley, *Stolen*, 172.

78. "The Bank of England's Special Liquidity Scheme," *Bank of England Quarterly Bulletin* (27 March 2012): 59, accessed 27 April 2022, https://www.bankofengland.co.uk/quarterly-bulletin/2012/q1/the-bank-of-englands-special-liquidity-scheme.

79. HM Treasury, "Mortgage Finance: Final Report and Recommendations, Sir James Crosby," accessed 27 April 2022, http://www.hm-treasury.gov.uk/d/pbr08_mortgagefinance_1010.pdf.

80. Nationwide Building Society, "Annual Percentage Change in UK House Prices."

81. Tooze, *Crashed*, 156.

82. Dorling, *All That Is Solid*, 2.

83. Anna Minton, *Big Capital: Who Is London For?* (Penguin UK, 2017), 9.

84. Office for National Statistics, "Index of Private Housing Rental Prices," accessed 27 April 2022, https://www.ons.gov.uk/datasets/index-private-housing -rental-prices/editions/time-series/versions/10.

85. Saunders, "Restoring a Nation of Home Owners," 70.

86. Saunders, "Restoring a Nation of Home Owners," 70–75.

87. Antony Seely et al., "Extending Home Ownership: Government Initiatives," House of Commons Library Research Briefings, 27 April 2022, 14, https:// commonslibrary.parliament.uk/research-briefings/sn03668/.

88. "George Osborne's Help to Buy Scheme 'a Moronic Policy,'" *Guardian*, 4 June 2013, https://www.theguardian.com/business/2013/jun/04/george-osborne-help -to-buy-moronic.

89. Patrick Collinson, "Help to Buy Has Mostly Helped Housebuilders Boost Profits," *Guardian*, 21 October 2017, https://www.theguardian.com/money/blog/2017/oct /21/help-to-buy-property-new-build-price-rise.

90. Department for Levelling Up, Housing and Communities, and Ministry of Housing, Communities and Local Government, "English Housing Survey Data on Tenure Trends and Cross Tenure Analysis," accessed 25 April 2022, https://www.gov .uk/government/statistical-data-sets/tenure-trends-and-cross-tenure-analysis.

91. 'Why Are More Young People Living with Their Parents? - Office for National Statistics,' accessed 27 April 2022, https://www.ons.gov.uk/ peoplepopulationandcommunity/birthsdeathsandmarriages/families/articles/whyarem oreyoungpeoplelivingwiththeirparents/2016-02-22.

92. "Tories Vote down Law Requiring Landlords Make Their Homes Fit for Human Habitation," *Independent*, 13 January 2016, https://www.independent.co.uk/news/uk /politics/tories-vote-down-law-requiring-landlords-make-their-homes-fit-for-human -habitation-a6809691.html.

93. Resolution Foundation, "Housing Outlook Q3 2021," accessed 27 April 2022, https://www.resolutionfoundation.org/publications/housing-outlook-q3-2021/.

Conclusion

Although we tend to think of the housing crisis as a phenomenon of the contemporary conjuncture, it has a long history. As this book has shown, there has never been a point in Britain when everyone has been able to realise their right to adequate housing. Nevertheless, there were periods in history when the realisation of this right was at least an objective of policy. Although always contested, across the mid-twentieth century, houses were seen not as assets but as homes that everyone had a right to. Through the provision of council housing, the regulation of the private rented sector and the expansion of owner occupation, an ever-increasing proportion of the population gained access to adequate housing. This was undermined at the end of the twentieth century as the Thatcher government progressively relieved the state of its responsibilities to house the people. These policies were largely confirmed by New Labour, who seemed unable or unwilling to eschew the view of housing as an asset. Although house price inflation has made many individuals very rich and played a vital role in sustaining the economy as wages and the reassurance of the welfare state were eroded, the remaking of housing as an asset is incompatible with both economic stability and the people's right to housing.

THE CONTEMPORARY CRISIS

Every sector is currently in crisis. Social housing is a shadow of its former self, decimated by Right to Buy and regeneration, and across the country waiting lists continue to grow. Those fortunate enough to get a council property encounter a government seemingly determined to punish them for this privilege. Whereas once lifetime tenure was understood to foster vital psychological security, today's tenants are given ever-shorter tenancies. Instead of the vision of high-quality and spacious accommodation that enabled a dignified life, today's tenants are financially penalised should their life course leave them with a spare bedroom. Local authorities have suffered massive cuts over the last decade, leaving them short of resources for maintenance.

Although the proportion of social housing in poor condition is far less than in the private sector, more than 200,000 now find themselves in council houses that fail to meet the decency standard. Those in stock transferred to housing associations fare little better, with 299,000 properties in the sector failing to meet this standard, despite the six-figure salaries common in the industry.[1]

In 2021, Robert Jenerick, then Housing Secretary, described the pay of housing association executives as "out of control" and urged the sector to go back to its "strong social and moral mission" and "take very seriously the interests of residents."[2] During their early history the mission to house the people animated associations, but in recent decades, under the pressure of policy reforms and reduced funding, housing associations have undergone a transformation akin to the building societies. They have assumed a more commercial character, raising capital on the markets, expanding into for-profit activities, storing large operational reserves and undergoing mergers which further remove them from the communities they are supposedly accountable to.[3] If housing associations are to again focus on their social mission, the funding systems that facilitated this need to be restored, but this seems unlikely in the current conjunction. When confronted with the proliferation of poor conditions in the social sector, Jenrick claimed, "This is nothing to do with government funding at all. This is about neglect. This is about a lack of compassion and poor management in a small number of councils and housing associations."[4] It is absurd to argue that this has nothing to do with the cuts local authorities have endured for more than a decade and the progressive removal of the funding that enabled housing associations to focus on their social priorities.

The decimation of social housing means that most have little choice but to rent privately. The sector has doubled in the new century, with around a fifth of the population now renting from private landlords. Across this period, rents have consistently risen. Social investigators in the nineteenth century were shocked to find that tenants paid as much as a third of their incomes in rent, but this is now the average amount that tenants spend. Low-income households spend more than 50 percent of their income on housing. Housing is judged to be affordable if it accounts for less than 30 percent of income, yet among those in the bottom 40 percent of the income distribution, more than two-thirds pay in excess of this; in London and the Southeast, this rises to more than 90 percent.[5] As well as countless individuals, the taxpayer has borne the cost of rising rents. More than a quarter of tenants receive housing benefit to assist with their rents.[6] Annual expenditure on housing benefit exceeds £20 billion, despite efforts to reduce it with the harsh benefits cap that displaced low-income households out of cities and other high rental areas.[7] One cannot help think that this money would be better spent building houses than lining landlords' pockets.

Despite high rents, tenants continue to endure poor housing conditions. The private rented sector has the highest proportion of properties that fail to meet the decency standard. While 23 percent of all privately rented households live in non-decent homes, this rises to 29 percent among those receiving housing benefit. Overcrowding remains persistent, and increased during the COVID pandemic, when 15 percent of households in the sector were judged to be overcrowded.[8] Although local authorities have some powers to enforce minimum standards, they do not have the resources to do this in practice. Living in overcrowded and poorly maintained housing has serious impacts on tenants' mental and physical health. Poor housing is estimated to cost the National Health Service at least £340 million a year.[9] These risks were underlined during the pandemic, when we saw a clear correlation between poor housing conditions and mortality and morbidity rates.[10]

Psychological harm is also done by the insecure tenancies that are the norm in the sector, where tenants can face rent increases or eviction with little notice. Eviction from the private rented sector is the leading cause of homelessness. In 2021, more than 274,000 people in England were homeless, including 126,000 children.[11] The vast majority are placed in temporary or emergency accommodation, largely provided by a multimillion-pound private industry. In 2020–2021, local authorities spent more than £1.4 billion on temporary accommodation. It costs considerably more to house people in temporary accommodation: each household moved into social housing saves councils around £7,760 a year. Even with this financial incentive, the lack of alternative housing means households languish in temporary accommodation for years and even decades.[12] During this time they endure some of the worst housing conditions, despite the profits made by the sector.[13]

One might think that owner occupation is the only sector immune from this generalised housing crisis. Homeowners have been the prime beneficiaries of housing policy for at least forty years. Those who bought in the mid- and late twentieth century were often helped to buy, received subsidies and tax relief on their mortgages and gained from a policy environment that took house price inflation as its measure of success. Not only have owners derived considerable profits from the increasing value of their homes, the low interest rates that have prevailed since the 1990s mean that on average owners spend proportionally less of their income on housing each month. While in the 1950s, both owners and tenants spent less than 10 percent of their income on housing, now, while tenants devote more than 30 percent of their income to housing, owners with mortgages spend just 18 percent.[14] This means that tenure itself has become a driver of inequality. Matthew Rognlie suggests that Thomas Piketty's book *Capital in the Twenty-First Century* might better be titled *Housing in the Twenty-First Century*, as he estimates that housing is responsible for 80 percent of the growth in inequality identified by Piketty.[15]

Homeowners are a diverse group. The situation of the 35 percent of households who own their homes outright, and have likely benefited from years
of house price inflation and the massive generational transfer of wealth this
entailed, is somewhat different to the million households who purchased
their first home in 2020–2021.[16] This again is a varied group, but many have
been allowed and incentivised to borrow far more than used to be considered
prudent to afford today's meteoric prices. This leaves them vulnerable to rising interest rates, which currently stand at historic lows. However, inflation
is once again stalking the economy, and interest rates are rising as a cost-of-
living crisis bites. While rates still have a long way to go to reach the levels
that placed so many households under strain at the end of the 1980s, many
today have borrowed far greater multiples of their income. Even if rates
do not return to these highs, the experience of subprime mortgagors in the
United States demonstrates the vulnerability of overextended borrowers and
the havoc this can cause in the wider economy. The global economy is no less
entwined with housing finance than it was in 2007 and the housing market no
more immune to crashing. It seems strange that house price inflation is not
viewed with more suspicion, given that cycles of booms and bust have led
to the housing market crashing three times in the last fifty years, each time
sending greater shockwaves across the economy.

The first step to moving beyond the current housing paradigm is to recognise the harms done by rising house prices, both to those who are unable to
afford adequate housing and to the stability of the national economy. Just as
general inflation is seen as a negative economic phenomenon, the same must
be the case for house price inflation. Dependence on house price inflation
might have been a quick way to paper over the cracks in Britain's postin-
dustrial economy, but it is not a prudent economic strategy in the long run.
The tendency towards boom and bust in the property market destabilises the
broader economy. House price inflation generates inequality, both between
tenures and between generations. Without significant wage increases, it
is hard to see how this cycle of generational wealth transfer can continue.
While those who own their homes outright might be buoyed consumers,
overindebted recent entrants to the market who have purchased at historically
low interest rates and look anxiously at each interest rate rise are far less
likely to be confident consumers. The economic rationale for housing policy
more broadly is also dubious. Billions are thrown away each year in housing
benefit and transferred to the range of providers that have emerged to profit
out of the state's withdrawal from housing. This money is better invested in
longer-term solutions to the housing crisis.

If the housing system isn't working for the economy, it certainly isn't
working for the people, for whom the struggle to house themselves becomes
more onerous each year. It ought to be a source of great national shame that

in one of the wealthiest countries in the world, so many do not have access to adequate housing, the foundation for physical and psychological well-being. To arrest this decline, we must once again place the right to housing at the centre of housing policy and pursue it with the same ambition as the architects of the programmes of the twentieth century which engendered such an improvement in people's standard of living.

THE POSSIBILITIES OF POLICY

This programme can be funded in a way that addresses the inequality that housing engenders and makes much-needed adjustments to the balance of taxation. As Piketty has highlighted, growing inequality since the late twentieth century has been fuelled by the rate of return from capital and assets, such as housing, far exceeding the growth in wages and output.[17] The taxation system does not reflect this reality. The vast bulk of tax revenues in Britain are generated from income, employment and consumption, while wealth and property are undertaxed. The main forms of property tax are stamp duty, a transaction tax paid by the purchaser rather than the seller, and council tax, which is based on 1991 property values, ignoring the house price inflation of the last thirty years. It is also paid by the occupier, rather than the owner, burdening renters rather than those who profit from increasing house values. There are other forms of taxation that would better address the inequality that property generates.

The arguments marshalled for land taxation still resonate today. Land is a finite resource and its ownership highly unequal. It was appropriated through theft, violence and domination, and amends must be made for the original and continuing dispossession of the people from this shared resource. Increases in value derive not from the labour of the owner but from the progress of society and the efforts of the community. As Winston Churchill argued in 1909, "Roads are made, streets are made, services are improved, electric light turns night into day, water is brought from reservoirs a hundred miles off in the mountains—and all the while the landlord sits still."[18] Local authorities are largely responsible for the provision and maintenance of our infrastructure, yet councils today face the same problem as their nineteenth-century predecessors, who found that the tax burden fell disproportionately on the poorer in society rather than the propertied interests that stood most to gain from urban investment. The regressive nature of council tax, the exclusion of landlords and, until recently, considerable discounts for second homeowners create the same issue today. The replacement of council tax with a form of land tax would prove a much fairer foundation for local taxation.

Similar arguments can be made about house price inflation. Generations of homeowners have benefitted from a policy environment that sought to maintain buoyant house prices. Aside from a little DIY, "what have these possessors done that this increase of wealth . . . should fall into their mouths as they sleep" instead of being applied to ameliorate the costs of house price inflation borne by the propertyless?[19] The solution to this is not a new tax but the removal of a tax exemption. Although in an ideal world we would want to move beyond the idea of houses as assets, while they are assets it is only right that they are treated as such and taxed appropriately. This means removing the exemption for primary residences under the capital gains tax so that houses are taxed in line with other assets.

Finally, we need to look at the issue of planning gain. When planning permission was introduced in the 1940s, it was accompanied by a betterment tax that captured the increase in value deriving from planning permission for the nation. Planning permission has never made any sense on its own, as it delivers an enormous and unearned windfall for the landowner. Critics claim that such a tax would disincentivise new construction, but this entirely depends on how it is implemented. We can take inspiration from the model that underlay the new towns, where planning gain was captured for the benefit of the community and vibrant town centres constructed with a mixture of public and private investment.

It is important to recognise that this is not a housing crisis we can build our way out of. There are now more houses per head than there were in the mid-twentieth century.[20] This is not a crisis of supply; it is a crisis of distribution, both in terms of people owning multiple properties, as second homes or as landlords, and of geographical distribution. Addressing the long-term regional imbalances in the national economy is a key step towards addressing the housing crisis, as is using the tax system to disincentivise the purchase of properties that are not primary residences. The impending environmental catastrophe should also make us pause before trying to build our way out of the crisis. Construction accounts for around 10 percent of the UK's carbon emissions.[21] For the last decades our skylines have been full of cranes hoisting new buildings into being, but the housing situation has deteriorated because construction is dictated by profit rather than housing needs. If we are to tackle the housing crisis while doing our best to avoid an environmental apocalypse, not only must we change the way we build but ensure that new building provides the homes we actually need rather than those that are most profitable.

What we need most is low-cost rental housing. The history of housing casts considerable doubt as to whether the private sector can ever provide this. From the nineteenth century to today, private landlords have been unable to extract sufficient profits to be able to offer decent and affordable housing to those with lower incomes. It was only when nonprofit organisations such as councils and housing associations stepped in that the housing needs of the people began to be met. Local authority housing must be a key component in any future housing programme. Across the mid-twentieth century, it significantly improved the standard of living for millions of people. The decision taken in the 1970s to address housing need through benefits rather than bricks and mortar has been a very costly failure. Billions of pounds of taxpayers' money each year is directed into private landlords' pockets instead of being invested in council housing which could house future generations. It is far more expensive for the state to pay people's rents in the private sector than to house them securely in council housing. In 2021, tenants in the private sector received on average £128 a week in housing benefit, compared to the £85 claimed by social tenants.[22] Council house building also benefits the economy. It is estimated that for every pound spent, more than £2 of economic output is generated, while more than half of expenditure is returned to the Treasury in tax revenues and benefit savings.[23] The benefits that derive from the psychic comfort people gain when they have decent and secure housing are immeasurable.

Council housing was not without its problems in the twentieth century. Throughout the twentieth century, policymakers faced a choice either to strive for the mixed communities they dreamt of or concentrate council housing on those most in need. Conservatives had always favoured the latter, seeing it as a residual tenure for only the poorest. Labour at first had a much bolder vision for all the people, but during the 1970s there was quite rightly outcry about the living conditions of those still waiting for council housing. In the context of the massive spending cuts made in the face of the economic crisis, Labour concluded that council housing must pragmatically be focused on those in greatest need. But as the incomes of the poorest fell away in the late twentieth century and unemployment grew to unprecedented levels, poverty and deprivation were concentrated on large estates. Today we face a similar dilemma to the 1970s where the scale of housing need makes it feel impossible to dream of building for all. If allocation is prioritised according to need, council housing must be dispersed on smaller sites, as this avoids social segregation, town clearances and building on greenfield sites on the outskirts of conurbations, all major issues in the twentieth century. Councils should consider buying up existing housing stock, either through the municipalisation of sections of the private rented sector or by purchasing owner occupied housing to prevent eviction of those facing repossession.

Other nonprofit organisations should also be supported to provide genuinely affordable housing. Funding should be restored for housing associations to enable them once again to focus on their social mission. Cooperatives too used to be able to access state funds. They have some advantages over housing associations. They not only provide residents with secure tenure and genuinely affordable rents but also control and agency over their living environments. It is the element of responsibility that goes along with agency that means cooperatives find support from across the political spectrum. Tantalisingly, they are a first step in overcoming the ideas of individual and absolute property ownership that underwrite the longer durée of the housing crisis. Despite having a long tradition of mutualism and cooperatives, the sector is underdeveloped in Britain compared to countries such as Sweden. In my city of Brighton, there is a small but vital cooperative sector, a remnant of the more supportive funding environment of the 1970s. I have seen the transformative effects that living in the cooperative sector can have on people's lives. Paying around a third of market rents, residents are liberated from the constant grind of having to scratch together enough to pay their rents and are free to pursue more worthwhile lives, whether in education or in more rewarding but less well-paid pursuits. Co-ops are a long way from images of past experiments in communal living. They offer a mix of private and shared spaces, depending on the needs of the households. Residents usually enjoy a much higher standard of living than tenants in the private sector. They not only have control over maintenance but often have generously sized communal spaces. Contrast this with the private sector, where many tenants find themselves in houses without any communal spaces bar a pokey kitchen, as every available room has been converted to a bedroom to maximise the rent. There remains much demand for cooperative housing in Brighton, but in a city that is seen as particularly profitable for property investment, co-ops struggle to compete against developers and investors.[24] For the sector to thrive, it needs first refusal on potential sites, as well as access to loans. In return for this relatively small assistance, cooperatives can build to the highest environmental standards and open their doors to people on the social housing waiting list, to ensure that they do not become the preserve of the newly precarious middle classes.

Building a vibrant not for profit rental sector will of course take time, and in the meantime, there are far too many people suffering through lack of adequate housing, particularly in the private rented sector. We need to act now to regulate the sector, to better balance the use rights of tenants to their home with the ownership rights of landlords. Tenants need greater security of tenure, while landlords must be mandated to let their properties in decent condition. Rent controls are also a sensible idea. Whenever discussed, they are framed as either bold and radical or reckless and dangerous, according to political persuasion. It seems to have been forgotten that they were the norm for much of the twentieth century, when they supported a growth in access to affordable housing. The history of rent controls in Britain is used as evidence by critics of rental regulation, who argue that controls led to a shrinkage of the sector and a decline in conditions.[25] Not only do such arguments ignore that contemporary forms of rent regulation are a lot more sophisticated than the crude cap introduced in 1915, they do not stand up to historical scrutiny. As this book has shown, conditions in the private rented sector were poor before controls were introduced and now, more than thirty years after deregulation, with rents higher than ever, the sector is still blighted by poor conditions. It would appear that however much profit landlords make, they are not inclined to invest to ensure their properties are in decent condition. Although the sector shrank during the time of controls, correlation is not causation. It is impossible to separate the impact of rent controls from the wider history of the sector, such as the enormous programme of slum clearances, the emergence of more profitable investment opportunities, the greater availability of housing finance and government subsidies that fuelled the rise of owner occupation. International comparisons also do not support the arguments against rent controls. Belgium, for example, has a relatively unregulated private rental sector, but the sector is shrinking and suffers from poor housing conditions. Germany, conversely, is highly regulated but the sector is large and stable, with tenants enjoying a high quality of accommodation.[26]

There is little radical or dangerous about rent regulation. It was the norm in Britain for most of the twentieth century and is still deployed successfully in countries around the world. One of the more surprising aspects of the Glasgow rent strike was the support the campaign received from several large local employers, who recognised the pressure that rising housing costs placed on wages.[27] Similar pressures are exerted today on private and public employers, who struggle to recruit and retain staff in high-rent areas. Controlling rents therefore offers wider economic benefits. Even if controls lead to a shrinkage of the sector, we have to ask if this is really such a bad thing, given its poor track record at providing people with decent, affordable and secure housing. The vast majority of properties lost from the private rented sector over the twentieth century became owner-occupied properties. The growth of homeownership and the decline of the private renting were the same process, yet you are unlikely to hear critics of rent controls bemoan the growth of owner-occupiers. Viewed in this light, rent controls look positively timid compared to the notion that we should leave something as essential as housing to the whims of the market, even when the harm this causes is more than evident.

While it is easy to come up with policy measures that would greatly alleviate the housing crisis that afflicts Britain and much of the world today, it is much harder to see how this could be achieved in the current conjuncture, where policy continues to move in the wrong direction. History is perhaps instructive here. The real and material improvements experienced across the mid-twentieth century were not benevolently bestowed by some caring government, nor simply accrued through a process of progressive policy evolution, but secured through collective struggle. Each chapter began with a story of everyday resistance, but these are just a few of the many episodes of popular struggle that litter the history of property and housing. History has an emotive power that we should not shy away from. We are both moved by the suffering endured by successive generations and inspired by the strength and heroism of struggle. Walter Benjamin stressed the vital power of such cross-temporal bonds of solidarity and obligation in inspiring and sustaining resistance, which he insisted was "nourished by the image of enslaved ances-tors rather than that of liberated grandchildren."[28] In our bleak times we can take sustenance from the actions of the women of Glasgow and all those who struggled valiantly to demand access to adequate housing. We owe them a debt of obligation to continue the struggle in the present.

We can also take more practical inspiration from the past. The shrewd campaign in Glasgow identified the forms of political, material and moral power ordinary people could exercise. This is admittedly harder outside the conditions of total war, but now, like then, landlords and other housing profi-teers are a relatively marginal class compared to those who struggle to house themselves. The settlement of the mid-twentieth century came undone as politicians feared the electoral consequences of not appealing to the growing numbers of owner-occupiers. Yet unless something changes, as Generation Rent ages, they will become the electoral majority. Politicians need to be taught to fear the consequences of standing idly by as the housing crisis wrecks ever more lives.

While it was the women of Glasgow who exerted crucial pressure on the government to act, the programme decided upon was shaped by the experi-ments developed over the preceding decades by radical councils in London, Liverpool and elsewhere. Key figures such as John Wheatley cut their teeth in municipal politics, and throughout its lifespan councils planned and controlled the housing programme. Housing is an issue that makes sense devolved to local authorities. They are best positioned to understand the particular housing needs of the communities to which they are democrati-cally accountable. They also own large amounts of land, control the planning process and, by borrowing against existing housing stock, can contribute to funding the housing drive. There is much appetite among councils to take a different approach to housing, but the crisis in funding and the national policy framework severely limits what they can do. Local authorities lack the powers and resources to properly regulate the private rented sector, and even when keen to rebuild their housing stock, they struggle to construct enough new homes to offset the continued loss of properties through Right to Buy.[29] While in the 1950s the Conservatives called for the private sector to be freed to meet the nation's housing needs, after decades of organising housing around the logics of the private market and seeing the harms this engenders, it is now time to set councils free so that they can fulfil their municipal responsibility to house the people.

We can get a sense of what might be possible by looking to Scotland. Responsibility for housing was devolved in 1999, and since then a different approach has developed. Right to Buy has been ended to safeguard existing council properties and there has been a great drive to restore social housing under the affordable housing programme. Between 2007 and 2020, Scotland built a third more affordable houses than England, and they credit this with the lower rates of child poverty that prevail north of the border. Moreover, unlike the programme in England, more than 65 percent of affordable homes built between 2016 and 2019 were for social rent. They have also built more than seven thousand midmarket rented homes for people who do not qualify for social housing but cannot afford private rents. Tenants in the private sector have been given far greater security of tenure with the ending of no-fault evictions. Control has also begun to be exerted over rents, with the introduction of rent pressure zones which empower local authorities to limit rent rises. A nationwide system of rent regulation is currently being developed. The tax system has been harnessed to discourage the scourges of buy-to-let investors and second-home buyers, who are liable for an additional 4 percent transaction tax. As transformative as these measures are, the government recognises that these are mere first steps and it sets out its future vision for housing policy in the recent *Housing to 2040*, pledging to organise housing around a set of principles. First is that everyone has the right to an adequate home: a secure, decent and affordable place where they want to live. Second is that the "housing system should supply high quality homes that are affordable for living in, to shift the balance away from the use of homes as a means to store wealth." And third is that government policy "should promote house price stability, to help underpin Scotland's standard of living and productivity and promote a Fairer Scotland." The government pledges to build one hundred thousand new affordable houses in the next decade while simultaneously taking massive steps to make the existing stock more energy efficient. Whilst such a project inevitably involves costs, these are presented not as a burden but as an investment in the future that will provide somewhere in the region of thirty-five thousand jobs as well increasing health, well-being and living standards.[30] This new approach demonstrates that it is possible to organise housing very differently and that benefits accrue when policy prioritises housing the people. Let's hope that events in Scotland once again have a wider disruptive effect.

NOTES

1. Ministry of Housing, Communities and Local Government, "English Housing Survey 2020 to 2021: Headline Report," annex table 2.3, accessed 25 April 2022, https://www.gov.uk/government/statistics/english-housing-survey-2020-to-2021-headline-report.

2. "Robert Jenrick Slams Housing Associations Bosses Pay as 'Out of Control,'" ITV News, 22 July 2021, https://www.itv.com/news/2021-07-22/exclusive-robert-jenrick-slams-housing-associations-and-bosses-pay-as-out-of-control.

3. Brian Lund, *Housing Politics in the United Kingdom: Power, Planning and Protest* (Policy Press, 2016), 197–99.

4. "Robert Jenrick Slams Housing Associations Bosses Pay as 'Out of Control.'"

5. Ministry of Housing, Communities and Local Government, "English Housing Survey, 2019 to 2020: Private Rented Sector," 18–19, accessed 25 April 2022, https://www.gov.uk/government/statistics/english-housing-survey-2019-to-2020-private-rented-sector.

6. Ministry of Housing, Communities and Local Government, "English Housing Survey 2020 to 2021," 20.

7. Department for Work and Pensions, "Benefit Expenditure and Caseload Tables 2021," accessed 25 April 2022, https://www.gov.uk/government/publications/benefit-expenditure-and-caseload-tables-2021.

8. Ministry of Housing, Communities and Local Government, "English Housing Survey, 2019 to 2020," 35, 3.

9. National Audit Office, "Regulation of Private Renting—National Audit Office (NAO) Report," 7, accessed 25 April 2022, https://www.nao.org.uk/report/regulation-of-private-renting/.

10. Nathaniel Barker, "The Housing Pandemic: Four Graphs Showing the Link between COVID-19 Deaths and the Housing Crisis," *Inside Housing*, 29 May 2020, https://www.insidehousing.co.uk/insight/insight/the-housing-pandemic-four-graphs-showing-the-link-between-covid-19-deaths-and-the-housing-crisis-66562.

11. Charlie Berry, "Homelessness in England 2021," Shelter England, accessed 25 April 2022, https://england.shelter.org.uk/professional_resources/policy_and_research/policy_library/homelessness_in_england_2021.

12. Cassie Barton and Wendy Wilson, "Households in Temporary Accommodation (England)," House of Commons Library Research Briefing, 25 April 2022, 5, https://commonslibrary.parliament.uk/research-briefings/sn02110/.

13. Oonagh Cousins, *Gutted, A Borough under Seige*, 2020, https://vimeo.com/436511659.

14. Ministry of Housing, Communities and Local Government, "English Housing Survey 2018 to 2019: Housing Costs and Affordability," 3, accessed 25 April 2022, https://www.gov.uk/government/statistics/english-housing-survey-2018-to-2019-housing-costs-and-affordability. Figures for 1953 calculated from A. Newell et al., "Living Standards of Working Households in Britain, 1904–1954" (UK Data Service, 2016), https://doi.org/10.5255/UKDA-SN-7916-1.

15. M. Rognlie, "A Note on Piketty and Diminishing Returns to Capital," Mimeo, Massachusetts Institute of Technology, 2014, 16–18.

16. Ministry of Housing, Communities and Local Government, "English Housing Survey 2020 to 2021," 3, 14.

17. Thomas Piketty, *Capital in the Twenty-First Century* (Harvard University Press, 2017).

18. Winston S. Churchill, *The People's Rights* (Rosetta Books, 2013), 118–19.

19. John Stuart Mill, "Advice to Land Reformers," in *Dissertations and Discussions* (H. Holt, 1875), 265.

20. Peter Saunders, "Restoring a Nation of Home Owners," Civitas: Institute for the Study of Civil Society, 12 June 2016, 42, http://civitas.org.ukhttps://www.civitas.org.uk/publications/restoring-a-nation-of-home-owners/.

21. "The Guardian View on Buildings: Out with the New! For the Planet's Sake," *Guardian*, 18 August 2021, https://www.theguardian.com/commentisfree/2021/aug/18/the-guardian-view-on-buildings-out-with-the-new-for-the-planets-sake.

22. Ministry of Housing, Communities and Local Government, "English Housing Survey 2020 to 2021," 20.

23. Matt Griffith and Pete Jeffreys, "Briefing: Solutions for the Housing Shortage," Shelter England, 8, accessed 25 April 2022, https://england.shelter.org.uk/professional_resources/policy_and_research/policy_library/briefing_solutions_for_the_housing_shortage.

24. Brighton and Hove Community Land Trust, accessed 25 April 2022, https://bhclt.org.uk/; CHIBAH—Co-Operative Housing in Brighton and Hove, accessed 25 April 2022, http://chibah.org/.

25. See critics referred to in Cassie Barton and Wendy Wilson, "Private Rented Housing: The Rent Control Debate," House of Commons Library Research Briefing, 25 April 2022, https://commonslibrary.parliament.uk/research-briefings/sn06760/.

26. Kathleen Scanlon and Ben Kochan, "Private Renting in Other Countries," in *Towards a Sustainable Private Rented Sector: The Lessons from Other Countries*, ed. Kathleen Scanlon and Ben Kochan (LSE London, London School of Economics and Political Science, 2011).

27. David Englander, *Landlord and Tenant in Urban Britain, 1838–1918* (Clarendon Press, 1983), 216–17.

28. Walter Benjamin, *Illuminations* (Random House, 2015), 252.

29. Brighton finally managed to build more than was sold in 2021, one of only a handful of authorities to do this. Olivia Marshall, "Brighton Council Replace More Council Houses Than Were Sold," *Argus*, 21 April 2021, https://www.theargus.co.uk/news/19248681.brighton-council-replace-council-houses-sold/.

30. Scottish Government, "Housing to 2040," accessed 25 April 2022, http://www.gov.scot/publications/housing-2040-2/; Audit Scotland, "Affordable Housing," accessed 25 April 2022, https://www.audit-scotland.gov.uk/publications/affordable-housing; Scottish Government, "Housing to 2040 Principles," http://www.gov.scot/publications/housing-2040-vision-principles/.

Bibliography

Audit Scotland. "Affordable Housing." Accessed 25 April 2022. https://www.audit -scotland.gov.uk/publications/affordable-housing.

Allan, C. M. "The Genesis of British Urban Redevelopment with Special Reference to Glasgow." *Economic History Review* 18, no. 3 (1965): 598–613. https://doi.org /10.2307/2592567.

Altholz, Josef L. *Selected Documents in Irish History*. Routledge, 2015.

Baldwin, Stanley. "Political Broadcasts." *Listener*, 30 October 1935.

Barker, Nathaniel. "The Housing Pandemic: Four Graphs Showing the Link between COVID-19 Deaths and the Housing Crisis." *Inside Housing*, 29 May 2020. https://www.insidehousing.co.uk/insight/insight/the-housing-pandemic-four-graphs -showing-the-link-between-covid-19-deaths-and-the-housing-crisis-66562.

Barton, Cassie, and Wendy Wilson. "Households in Temporary Accommodation (England)." House of Commons Library Research Briefing, 25 April 2022. https://commonslibrary.parliament.uk/research-briefings/sn02110/.

———. "Private Rented Housing: The Rent Control Debate." House of Commons Library Research Briefing, 25 April 2022. https://commonslibrary.parliament.uk/ research-briefings/sn06760/.

Bateman, John. *The Acre-Ocracy of England. A List of All Owners of Three Thousand Acres and Upwards. . . .* Pickering, 1876.

Benjamin, Walter. *Illuminations*. Random House, 2015.

Berry, Charlie. "Homelessness in England 2021." Shelter England. Accessed 25 April 2022. https://england.shelter.org.uk/professional_resources/policy_and_research/ policy_library/homelessness_in_england_2021.

"Blair's Speech: Single Mothers Won't Be Forced to Take Work." BBC Politics 97. Accessed 26 April 2022. https://www.bbc.co.uk/news/special/politics97/news/06 /0602/blair.shtml.

Blakeley, Grace. *Stolen: How to Save the World from Financialisation*. Repeater, 2019.

Boddy, Martin. *The Building Societies*. Macmillan, 1980.

———. "Financial Deregulation and UK Housing Finance: Government-building Society Relations and the Building Societies Act, 1986." *Housing Studies* 4, no. 2 (1 April 1989): 92–104. https://doi.org/10.1080/02673038908720647.

Boughton, John. "The Aylesbury Estate, Southwark: 'All That Is Left of the High Hopes of the Post-War Planners Is Derelict Concrete.'" *Municipal Dreams* (blog), 7 January 2014. https://municipaldreams.wordpress.com/2014/01/07/the -aylesbury-estate-southwark-where-all-that-is-left-of-the-high-hopes-of-the-post -war-planners-is-derelict-concrete/.

———. "Clay Cross Council: 'Doing Our Job—and That's to Help the Working Class, the Cream of the Nation.'" *Municipal Dreams* (blog), 31 March 2015. https: //municipaldreams.wordpress.com/2015/03/31/clay_cross_part_two/.

———. *Municipal Dreams: The Rise and Fall of Council Housing.* Verso Books, 2018.

Cage, R. A. "Infant Mortality and Housing: Twentieth Century Glasgow." *Scottish Economic and Social History* 14, no. 1 (1 May 1994): 77–92. https://doi.org/10 .3366/sesh.1994.14.14.77.

Cameron, Ewen. "Setting the Heather on Fire: The Land Question in Scotland, 1850–1914." In *The Land Question in Britain, 1750–1950*, edited by M. Cragoe and P. Readman. Palgrave Macmillan UK, 2010.

Castells, Manuel. *The City and the Grassroots: A Cross-Cultural Theory of Urban Social Movements.* University of California Press, 1983.

Chatterjee, Partha. "The Colonial State and Peasant Resistance in Bengal 1920–1947." *Past and Present*, no. 110 (1986): 169–204.

Child, Phil. "Landlordism, Rent Regulation and the Labour Party in Mid-Twentieth Century Britain, 1950–64." *Twentieth Century British History* 29, no. 1 (1 March 2018): 79–103. https://doi.org/10.1093/tcbh/hwx036.

Churchill, Winston S. "Election Address, Cardiff, 8 February 1950." In *In the Balance*. RosettaBooks, 2014.

———. *The People's Rights.* Rosetta Books, 2013.

Cleary, E. J. *The Building Society Movement.* Elek Books, 1965.

Cobham, David. "The Lawson Boom: Excessive Depreciation versus Financial Liberalisation." *Financial History Review* 4, no. 1 (April 1997): 69–90. https://doi .org/10.1017/S0968565000000846.

Coleman, Alice. *Utopia on Trial: Vision and Reality in Planned Housing.* H. Shipman, 1985.

Collini, Stefan. *Public Moralists: Political Thought and Intellectual Life in Britain.* Clarendon Press, 1991.

Collinson, Patrick. "Help to Buy Has Mostly Helped Housebuilders Boost Profits." *Guardian*, 21 October 2017. https://www.theguardian.com/money/blog/2017/oct /21/help-to-buy-property-new-build-price-rise.

"The Bank of England's Special Liquidity Scheme." *Bank of England Quarterly Bulletin* (27 March 2012): 57–66. Accessed 27 April 2022. https://www .bankofengland.co.uk/quarterly-bulletin/2012/q1/the-bank-of-englands-special -liquidity-scheme.

"Competition and Credit Control: Text of a Consultative Document Issued on 14th May 1971 as a Basis for Discussion with Banks and Finance Houses." *Bank of England Quarterly Bulletin* 11, no. 2 (1 June 1971): 189–93.

Copley, Jack. "Financial Deregulation and the Role of Statecraft: Lessons from Britain's 1971 Competition and Credit Control Measures." *New Political Economy*

22, no. 6 (2 November 2017): 692–708. https://doi.org/10.1080/13563467.2017 .1311849.

Cousins, Oonagh. *Gutted, A Borough under Seige*, 2020. https://vimeo.com /436511659.

Craig, Maggie. *When the Clyde Ran Red: A Social History of Red Clydeside*. Birlinn, 2018.

Crosland, Anthony. *The Conservative Enemy: A Programme of Radical Reform for the 1960s*. Schocken Books, 1962.

———. *The Future of Socialism*. J. Cape, 1961.

Crouch, Colin. "Privatised Keynesianism: An Unacknowledged Policy Regime." *British Journal of Politics and International Relations* 11, no. 3 (2009): 382–99. https://doi.org/10.1111/j.1467-856X.2009.00377.x.

Curtis, Lewis Perry. *Coercion and Conciliation in Ireland 1880–1892*. Princeton University Press, 2015.

Damer, Sean. "State, Class and Housing." In *Housing, Social Policy and the State*, edited by Joseph Melling. Croom Helm, 1980.

Daunton, Martin J. *A Property-Owning Democracy? Housing in Britain*. Faber, 1987.

———. *Councillors and Tenants: Local Authority Housing in English Cities, 1919–1939*. Leicester University Press, 1984.

———. *House and Home in the Victorian City: Working-Class Housing, 1580–1914*. Edward Arnold, 1983.

Davies, Aled. "'Right to Buy': The Development of a Conservative Housing Policy, 1945–1980." *Contemporary British History* 27, no. 4 (1 December 2013): 421–44. https://doi.org/10.1080/13619462.2013.824660.

Davies, Aled, Ben Jackson, and Florence Sutcliffe-Braithwaite. *The Neoliberal Age? Britain since the 1970s*. UCL Press, 2021.

Department for Levelling Up, Housing and Communities, and Ministry of Housing, Communities and Local Government. "English Housing Survey Data on Tenure Trends and Cross Tenure Analysis." Accessed 25 April 2022. https://www.gov.uk/ government/statistical-data-sets/tenure-trends-and-cross-tenure-analysis.

Department for Work and Pensions. "Benefit Expenditure and Caseload Tables 2021." Accessed 25 April 2022. https://www.gov.uk/government/publications/benefit -expenditure-and-caseload-tables-2021.

Department of Environment. "Fair Deal for Housing," 1971. Cmnd. 4728. Parliamentary Papers.

———. "Housing Policy," 1977. Cmnd. 6851. Parliamentary Papers.

Dorling, Danny. *All That Is Solid: How the Great Housing Disaster Defines Our Times, and What We Can Do About It*. Penguin UK, 2014.

Douglas, Roy. *Land, People and Politics: A History of the Land Question in the United Kingdom, 1878–1952*. St. Martin's Press, 1976.

Eden, Anthony. *Freedom and Order: Selected Speeches, 1939–1946*. Houghton Mifflin, 1948.

Englander, David. *Landlord and Tenant in Urban Britain, 1838–1918*. Clarendon Press, 1983.

————. *Landlord and Tenant in Urban Britain: The Politics of Housing Reform, 1838–1924*. PhD dissertation, University of Warwick, 1979. http://wrap.warwick .ac.uk/2821/.

Finlayson, Alan. "Financialisation, Financial Literacy and Asset-Based Welfare." *British Journal of Politics and International Relations* 11, no. 3 (1 August 2009): 400–21. https://doi.org/10.1111/j.1467-856X.2009.00378.x.

Fraser, William Hamish, and Irene Maver. *Glasgow: Volume II: 1830–1912.* Manchester University Press, 1996.

Gauldie, Enid. *Cruel Habitations: A History of Working-Class Housing, 1780–1918.* Barnes and Noble, 1974.

Gazeley, Ian, Andrew Newell, and P. Scott. "Why Was Urban Overcrowding Much More Severe in Scotland than in the Rest of the British Isles? Evidence from the First (1904) Official Household Expenditure Survey." *European Review of Economic History* 15, no. 1 (2011): 127–51.

Gentle, Christopher, Daniel Dorling, and James Comford. "Negative Equity and British Housing in the 1990s: Cause and Effect." *Urban Studies* 31, no. 2 (1 March 1994): 181–99. https://doi.org/10.1080/00420989420080191.

"George Osborne's Help to Buy Scheme 'a Moronic Policy." *Guardian*, 4 June 2013. https://www.theguardian.com/business/2013/jun/04/george-osborne-help-to-buy -moronic.

George, Henry. *Henry George's Writings on the United Kingdom*. Emerald Group Publishing, 2002.

Glasgow Labour History Workshop. *The Singer Strike Clydebank, 1911*. Clydebank District Library, 1989.

Gosling, Ray. *St Ann's*. Civic Trust, 1967.

Gotham, Kevin Fox. "Creating Liquidity out of Spatial Fixity: The Secondary Circuit of Capital and the Subprime Mortgage Crisis." *International Journal of Urban and Regional Research* 33, no. 2 (2009): 355–71. https://doi.org/10.1111/j.1468-2427 .2009.00874.x.

Gray, Neil. *Rent and Its Discontents: A Century of Housing Struggle*. Rowman and Littlefield, 2018.

Green, E. H. H. *The Crisis of Conservatism: The Politics, Economics and Ideology of the Conservative Party, 1880–1914*. Routledge, 2005.

Griffith, Matt, and Pete Jeffreys. "Briefing: Solutions for the Housing Shortage." Shelter England. Accessed 25 April 2022. https://england.shelter.org.uk/ professional_resources/policy_and_research/policy_library/briefing_solutions_for _the_housing_shortage.

"The Guardian View on Buildings: Out with the New! For the Planet's Sake." *Guardian*, 18 August 2021. https://www.theguardian.com/commentisfree/2021/aug /18/the-guardian-view-on-buildings-out-with-the-new-for-the-planets-sake.

Guinnane, Timothy W., and Ronald I. Miller. "The Limits to Land Reform: The Land Acts in Ireland, 1870–1909." *Economic Development and Cultural Change* 45, no. 3 (1997): 591–612. https://doi.org/10.1086/452292.

Hall, Stuart, Chas Critcher, Tony Jefferson, Brian Roberts, and John Clarke. *Policing the Crisis: Mugging, the State, and Law and Order*. Macmillan Education UK, 1978.

Harman, Mark. "The 1976 UK-IMF Crisis: The Markets, the Americans, and the IMF." *Contemporary British History* 11, no. 3 (2008): 1–17. Accessed 26 April 2022. https://www.tandfonline.com/doi/abs/10.1080/13619469708581446.

Harris, Jose. *The Penguin Social History of Britain: Private Lives, Public Spirit: Britain 1870–1914*. Penguin UK, 1994.

Harris, Nigel. *Competition and the Corporate Society: British Conservatives, the State and Industry 1945–1964*. Routledge, 2013.

Heim, Carol E. "The Treasury as Developer-Capitalist? British New Town Building in the 1950s." *Journal of Economic History* 50, no. 4 (1990): 903–24.

HM Treasury. "Mortgage Finance: Final Report and Recommendations, Sir James Crosby." Accessed 27 April 2022. http://www.hm-treasury.gov.uk/d/pbr08_mortgagefinance_1010.pdf.

Holmans, Alan. "Historical Statistics of Housing in Britain." Cambridge Centre for Housing and Planning Research, 22 April 2015. https://www.cchpr.landecon.cam.ac.uk/Research/Start-Year/2005/Other-Publications/Historical-Statistics-of-Housing-in-Britain.

Howkins, Alun. "From Diggers to Dongas: The Land in English Radicalism, 1649–2000." *History Workshop Journal*, no. 54 (2002): 1–23.

———. *Poor Labouring Men: Rural Radicalism in Norfolk, 1872–1923*. Routledge and Kegan Paul, 1985.

Inter-Departmental Committee on Physical Deterioration. "Report of the Inter-Departmental Committee on Physical Deterioration," 1904. CD. 2175. Parliamentary Papers.

Jackson, Ben. "Revisionism Reconsidered: 'Property-Owning Democracy' and Egalitarian Strategy in Post-War Britain." *Twentieth Century British History* 16, no. 4 (1 January 2005): 416–40. https://doi.org/10.1093/tcbh/hwi053.

Jacobs, Jane M., and Loretta Lees. "Defensible Space on the Move: Revisiting the Urban Geography of Alice Coleman." *International Journal of Urban and Regional Research* 37, no. 5 (2013): 1559–83. https://doi.org/10.1111/1468-2427.12047.

Jacobs, K., J. Kemeny, and T. Manzi. "Privileged or Exploited Council Tenants? The Discursive Change in Conservative Housing Policy from 1972 to 1980." *Policy and Politics* 31, no. 3 (1 July 2003): 307–20. https://doi.org/10.1332/030557303322034965.

Jay, Douglas. *Socialism in the New Society*. Longmans, 1962.

Jones, Ben. "Slum Clearance, Privatization and Residualization: The Practices and Politics of Council Housing in Mid-Twentieth-Century England." *Twentieth Century British History* 21, no. 4 (2010): 510–39. https://doi.org/10.1093/tcbh/hwq025.

———. "The Uses of Nostalgia." *Cultural and Social History* 7, no. 3 (1 September 2010): 355–74. https://doi.org/10.2752/147800410X12714191853346.

———. *The Working Class in Mid-Twentieth-Century England: Community, Identity and Social Memory*. Manchester University Press, 2018.

Jones, Colin, and Alan Murie. *The Right to Buy: Analysis and Evaluation of a Housing Policy*. John Wiley and Sons, 2008.

Jones, Daniel Stedman. *Masters of the Universe: Hayek, Friedman, and the Birth of Neoliberal Politics—Updated Edition*. Princeton University Press, 2014.

Jones, Gareth Stedman. *Outcast London: A Study in the Relationship between Classes in Victorian Society*. Verso Books, 2014.

Jones, Harriet. *The Conservative Party and the Welfare State 1942–1955*. PhD dissertation, London School of Economics and Political Science (University of London), 1992.

———. "'This Is Magnificent!'": 300,000 Houses a Year and the Tory Revival after 1945." *Contemporary British History* 14, no. 1 (1 March 2000): 99–121. https://doi .org/10.1080/13619460008581574.

Kemp, Peter A., and Tony Crook. *Transforming Private Landlords: Housing, Markets and Public Policy*. John Wiley and Sons, 2011.

King, Peter. *Crime and Law in England, 1750–1840: Remaking Justice from the Margins*. Cambridge University Press, 2006.

———. "Legal Change, Customary Right, and Social Conflict in Late Eighteenth-Century England: The Origins of the Great Gleaning Case of 1788." *Law and History Review* 10, no. 1 (ed 1992): 1–31. https://doi.org/10.2307/743812.

Land Tenure Reform Association and John Stuart Mill. *Programme of the Land Tenure Reform Association*. Longmans, Green, Reader, and Dyer, 1871.

Lawrence, Jon. "Class and Gender in the Making of Urban Toryism, 1880–1914." *English Historical Review* 108, no. 428 (1 July 1993): 629–52. https://doi.org/10 .1093/ehr/CVIII.428.629.

———. "Inventing the Traditional Working Class: A Re-Analysis of Interview Notes from Young and Willmott's Family Kinship in East London." *Historical Journal* 59, no. 2 (June 2016): 567–93. https://doi.org/10.1017/S0018246X15000515.

Leather, Philip, and Brendan Nevin. "The Housing Market Renewal Programme: Origins, Outcomes and the Effectiveness of Public Policy Interventions in a Volatile Market." *Urban Studies* 50, no. 5 (1 April 2013): 856–75. https://doi.org /10.1177/0042098012449667.

Lees, Loretta. "The Urban Injustices of New Labour's 'New Urban Renewal': The Case of the Aylesbury Estate in London." *Antipode* 46, no. 4 (2014): 921–47. https: //doi.org/10.1111/anti.12020.

Lees, Loretta, and Hannah White. "The Social Cleansing of London Council Estates: Everyday Experiences of 'Accumulative Dispossession.'" *Housing Studies* 35, no. 10 (25 November 2020): 1701–22. https://doi.org/10.1080/02673037.2019 .1680814.

Leyshon, Andrew, and Shaun French. "'We All Live in a Robbie Fowler House': The Geographies of the Buy to Let Market in the UK." *British Journal of Politics and International Relations* 11, no. 3 (1 August 2009): 438–60. https://doi.org/10.1111 /j.1467-856X.2009.00381.x.

Linklater, Andro. *Owning the Earth: The Transforming History of Land Ownership*. A&C Black, 2014.

Locke, John. "Of Property." In *Locke: Political Writings*, edited by. Hackett Publishing, 2003.

Lord, Chris, James Lloyd, and Matt Barnes. "Whose Home? Understanding Landlords and Their Effect on Public Policy." Strategic Society, 4 July 2013. https://strategicsociety.org.uk/whose-home-understanding-landlords-and-their-effect-on-public-policy/.

Lowe, Stuart. *The Housing Debate*. Policy Press, 2011.

Lund, Brian. *Housing Politics in the United Kingdom: Power, Planning and Protest*. Policy Press, 2016.

———. *Understanding Housing Policy*. Policy Press, 2011.

Malpass, Peter. "The Road from Clay Cross." In *Built to Last? Reflections on British Housing Policy*, edited by John Goodwin and Carol Grant. ROOF Magazine, 1997.

———. "The Unravelling of Housing Policy in Britain." *Housing Studies* 11, no. 3 (1 July 1996): 459–70. https://doi.org/10.1080/02673039608720868.

Marshall, Olivia. "Brighton Council Replace More Council Houses Than Were Sold." *Argus*, 21 April 2021. https://www.theargus.co.uk/news/19248681.brighton-council-replace-council-houses-sold/.

Massey, Doreen B., and Alejandrina Catalano. *Capital and Land: Landownership by Capital in Great Britain*. E. Arnold, 1978.

Melling, Joseph. "Clydeside Housing and the Evolution of State Rent Control." In *Housing, Social Policy and the State*, edited by Joseph Melling. Croom Helm, 1980.

———. *Rent Strikes: Peoples' Struggle for Housing in West Scotland, 1890–1916*. Polygon Books, 1983.

Merrett, Stephen. *State Housing in Britain*. Routledge and Kegan Paul, 1979.

Merrett, Stephen, and Fred Gray. *Owner-Occupation in Britain*. Routledge and Kegan Paul, 1982.

Mill, John Stuart. "Advice to Land Reformers." In *Dissertations and Discussions*. H. Holt, 1875.

———. "The Condition of Ireland." *Morning Chronicle*, 13 October 1846.

———. *England and Ireland*. Longmans, Green, Reader, and Dyer, 1868.

———. "Leslie on the Land Question." *Fortnightly Review*, 1870.

———. *Principles of Political Economy: With Some of Their Applications to Social Philosophy*. Longmans, Green, Reader, and Dyer, 1866.

Ministry of Housing and Local Government. "Houses the Next Step," 1953. Cmd. 8996. Parliamentary Papers.

———. "Housing in England and Wales," 1961. Cmnd. 1290. Parliamentary Papers.

———. "Old Houses into New," 1968. Cmd. 3602. Parliamentary Papers.

———. "The Housing Programme," 1965. Cmnd. 2838. Parliamentary Papers.

Ministry of Housing, Communities and Local Government. "English Housing Survey 2018 to 2019: Housing Costs and Affordability." Accessed 25 April 2022. https://www.gov.uk/government/statistics/english-housing-survey-2018-to-2019-housing-costs-and-affordability.

———. "English Housing Survey, 2019 to 2020: Private Rented Sector." Accessed 25 April 2022. https://www.gov.uk/government/statistics/english-housing-survey -2019-to-2020-private-rented-sector.

———. "English Housing Survey 2020 to 2021: Headline Report." Accessed 25 April 2022. https://www.gov.uk/government/statistics/english-housing-survey -2020-to-2021-headline-report.

Minton, Anna. *Big Capital: Who Is London For?* Penguin UK, 2017.

———. *Ground Control: Fear and Happiness in the Twenty-First-Century City.* Penguin UK, 2012.

More, Thomas. *Utopia.* Wordsworth Editions, 1997.

National Audit Office. "Introduction to Asset-Backed Securities," November 2016. https://www.nao.org.uk/wp-content/uploads/2016/07/Introduction-to-asset-backed -securities.pdf.

———. "Regulation of Private Renting—National Audit Office (NAO) Report." Accessed 25 April 2022. https://www.nao.org.uk/report/regulation-of-private -renting/.

Nationwide Building Society. "Annual Percentage Change in UK House Prices." Accessed 27 April 2022. https://www.nationwidehousepriceindex.co.uk/resources/ chart-data-download-annual-percentage-change-in-uk-house-prices.

Nevitt, Adela Adam. *Housing, Taxation and Subsidies: A Study of Housing in the United Kingdom.* Nelson, 1966.

Newby, Dr Andrew. *Ireland, Radicalism, and the Scottish Highlands, c.1870–1912.* Edinburgh University Press, 2007.

Newell, A., J. Walker, M. Hawkins, P. Scott, and I. Gazeley. "Living Standards of Working Households in Britain, 1904–1954." UK Data Service, 2016. https://doi .org/10.5255/UKDA-SN-7916-1.

Newton, Scott. "The Sterling Devaluation of 1967, the International Economy and Post-War Social Democracy." *English Historical Review* 125, no. 515 (1 August 2010): 912–45. https://doi.org/10.1093/ehr/ceq164.

Nicholls, Sian. "The Construction of National Identity." In *The Conservatives and British Society, 1880–1990*, edited by Martin Francis and Ina Zweiniger-Bargielowska. University of Wales Press, 1996.

"1951 Conservative Party General Election Manifesto." Accessed 25 April 2022. http: //www.conservativemanifesto.com/1951/1951-conservative-manifesto.shtml.

"1959 Labour Party Election Manifesto." Accessed 26 April 2022. http://www.labour -party.org.uk/manifestos/1959/1959-labour-manifesto.shtml.

"October 1974 Conservative Party Manifesto." Accessed 26 April 2022. http:// www.conservativemanifesto.com/1974/Oct/october-1974-conservative-manifesto .shtml.

Offer, Avner. *Property and Politics 1870–1914: Landownership, Law, Ideology and Urban Development in England.* Cambridge University Press, 1981.

Office for National Statistics. "Household Debt: Wealth in Great Britain." Accessed 25 April 2022. https://www.ons.gov.uk/peoplepopulationandcommunity/ personalandhouseholdfinances/incomeandwealth/datasets/householddebtwealthin greatbritain.

———. "Index of Private Housing Rental Prices." Accessed 27 April 2022. https://www.ons.gov.uk/datasets/index-private-housing-rental-prices/edition/time-series/versions/10.

———. "LFS: Unemployed: UK: All: Aged 16+: 000s: SA: Annual=4 Quarter Average." Accessed 27 April 2022. https://www.ons.gov.uk/employmentandlabourmarket/peoplenotinwork/unemployment/timeseries/mgsc/unem.

———. "Why Are More Young People Living with Their Parents?" Accessed 27 April 2022. https://www.ons.gov.uk/peoplepopulationandcommunity/birthsdeathsandmarriages/families/articles/whyaremoreyoungpeoplelivingwiththeirparents/2016-02-22.

Office of the Deputy Prime Minister. *Sustainable Communities: Homes for All.* Stationery Office, 2005.

Packer, Ian. *Lloyd George, Liberalism and the Land: The Land Issue and Party Politics in England, 1906–1914.* Boydell and Brewer, 2001.

Park, K-Sue. "Money, Mortgages, and the Conquest of America." *Law and Social Inquiry* 41, no. 4 (ed 2016): 1006–35. https://doi.org/10.1111/lsi.12222.

Pawley, Martin. *Home Ownership.* Architectural Press, 1978.

Piketty, Thomas. *Capital in the Twenty-First Century.* Harvard University Press, 2017.

"Post-Mortem on Voting at the Election." *Quarterly Review* 284, no. 567 (1946):

Priest, Claire. "Creating an American Property Law: Alienability and Its Limits in American History." *Harvard Law Review* 120, no. 2 (2006): 385–459.

Ray, Ratna, and Rajat Ray. "Zamindars and Jotedars: A Study of Rural Politics in Bengal." *Modern Asian Studies* 9, no. 1 (1975): 81–102.

Reid, Margaret. *The Secondary Banking Crisis, 1973–75: Its Causes and Course.* Springer, 1982.

Rendell, Jane. "'Arry's Bar: Condensing and Displacing on the Aylesbury Estate." *Journal of Architecture* 22, no. 3 (3 April 2017): 532–54. https://doi.org/10.1080/13602365.2017.1310125.

"Report of the Commissioners on Benefit Building Societies, Part I," 1872. C. 514. Parliamentary Papers.

Resolution Foundation. "Housing Outlook Q3 2021." Accessed 27 April 2022. https://www.resolutionfoundation.org/publications/housing-outlook-q3-2021/.

"Robert Jenrick Slams Housing Associations Bosses Pay as 'Out of Control.'" ITV News, 22 July 2021. https://www.itv.com/news/2021-07-22/exclusive-robert-jenrick-slams-housing-associations-and-bosses-pay-as-out-of-control.

Rodger, Richard. *Housing in Urban Britain 1780–1914.* Cambridge University Press, 1995.

Rognlie, M. "A Note on Piketty and Diminishing Returns to Capital." Mimeo, Massachusetts Institute of Technology, 2014.

Rolnik, Raquel. "Report of the Special Rapporteur on Adequate Housing as a Component of the Right to an Adequate Standard of Living, and on the Right to Non-Discrimination in This Context," 30 December 2013. https://digitallibrary.un.org/record/766907.

———. *Urban Warfare: Housing under the Empire of Finance.* Verso Books, 2019.

Romyn, Michael. "The Heygate: Community Life in an Inner-City Estate, 1974–2011." *History Workshop Journal* 81, no. 1 (1 April 2016): 197–230. https://doi.org/10.1093/hwj/dbw013.

Ronald, R. *The Ideology of Home Ownership: Homeowner Societies and the Role of Housing.* Springer, 2008.

Salisbury, Lord. "Disintegration." *Spectator*, 20 October 1883. http://archive.spectator.co.uk/article/20th-october-1883/5/-disintegration.

Saunders, Peter. "Restoring a Nation of Home Owners." Civitas: Institute for the Study of Civil Society, 12 June 2016. http://civitas.org.ukhttps://www.civitas.org.uk/publications/restoring-a-nation-of-home-owners/.

Scanlon, Kathleen, and Ben Kochan. "Private Renting in Other Countries." In *Towards a Sustainable Private Rented Sector: The Lessons from Other Countries*, edited by Kathleen Scanlon and Ben Kochan. LSE London, London School of Economics and Political Science, 2011.

Scott, Peter. *The Making of the Modern British Home: The Suburban Semi and Family Life between the Wars.* Oxford University Press, 2013.

———. "The New Alchemy: Veblen's Theory of Crisis and the 1974 British Property and Secondary Banking Crisis." *Journal of Economic Issues* 30, no. 1 (1 March 1996): 1–11. https://doi.org/10.1080/00213624.1996.11505763.

———. *The Property Masters: A History of the British Commercial Property Sector.* Taylor and Francis, 1996.

Scott, Peter, and Lucy Ann Newton. "Advertising, Promotion, and the Rise of a National Building Society Movement in Interwar Britain." *Business History* 54, no. 3 (1 June 2012): 399–423. https://doi.org/10.1080/00076791.2011.638489.

Scottish Government. "Housing to 2040." Accessed 25 April 2022. http://www.gov.scot/publications/housing-2040-2/.

———. "Housing to 2040 Principles." Accessed 25 April 2022. http://www.gov.scot/publications/housing-2040-vision-principles/.

Seabrooke, Leonard, and H. Schwartz. *The Politics of Housing Booms and Busts.* Springer, 2009.

Seely, Antony, Cassie Barton, Hannah Cromarty, and Wendy Wilson. "Extending Home Ownership: Government Initiatives." House of Commons Library Research Briefings, 27 April 2022. https://commonslibrary.parliament.uk/research-briefings/sn03668/.

Skelton, Noel. "Constructive Conservatism." *Spectator*, 28 April 1923.

———. "Constructive Conservativism III. Problem and Principle." *Spectator*, 12 May 1923.

———. "Constructive Conservativism IV. Democracy Stabilised." *Spectator*, 19 May 1923.

Smith,. "No Welcome Home." In *Built to Last? Reflections on British Housing Policy*, edited by John Goodwin and Carol Grant. ROOF Magazine, 1997.

Smith, Susan J., and Beverley A. Searle. *The Blackwell Companion to the Economics of Housing: The Housing Wealth of Nations.* John Wiley and Sons, 2010.

Speight, George. *Building Society Behaviour and the Mortgage Lending Market in the Interwar Period: Risk-Taking by Mutual Institutions and the Interwar House-Building Boom*. PhD dissertation, University of Oxford, 2000.

Steele, E. D. "J. S. Mill and the Irish Question: Reform, and the Integrity of the Empire, 1865–1870." *Historical Journal* 13, no. 3 (1970): 419–50.

Stephens, Mark. "Mortgage Market Deregulation and Its Consequences." *Housing Studies* 22, no. 2 (1 March 2007): 201–20. https://doi.org/10.1080/02673030601132797.

Stockhammer, Engelbert. "Neoliberal Growth Models, Monetary Union and the Euro Crisis. A Post-Keynesian Perspective." *New Political Economy* 21, no. 4 (3 July 2016): 365–79. https://doi.org/10.1080/13563467.2016.1115826.

Sullivan, Alexander Martin. *New Ireland*. S. Low, Marston, Searle, and Rivington, 1877.

Swenarton, Mark. *Homes Fit for Heroes: The Politics and Architecture of Early State Housing in Britain*. Heinemann Educational Books, 1981.

Thatcher, Margaret. "Written Statement on Housing," 27 September 1974. https://www.margaretthatcher.org/document/102411.

Thompson, E. P. *Customs in Common: Studies in Traditional Popular Culture*. New Press/ORIM, 2015.

———. *The Making of the English Working Class*. Penguin Books, 2013.

Thomson, F. M. L. "Cobden, Free Trade in Land, and Road to the Abbey National." In *Rethinking Nineteenth-Century Liberalism: Richard Cobden Bicentenary Essays*, edited by Anthony Howe and Simon Morgan. Routledge, 2006.

Thornton, William Thomas. *A Plea for Peasant Proprietors: With the Outlines of a Plan for Their Establishment in Ireland*. John Murray, 1848.

Tooze, Adam. *Crashed: How a Decade of Financial Crises Changed the World*. Penguin UK, 2018.

"Tories Vote down Law Requiring Landlords Make Their Homes Fit for Human Habitation," *Independent*, 13 January 2016. https://www.independent.co.uk/news/uk/politics/tories-vote-down-law-requiring-landlords-make-their-homes-fit-for-human-habitation-a6809691.html.

Toye, Richard. "Winston Churchill's 'Crazy Broadcast': Party, Nation, and the 1945 Gestapo Speech." *Journal of British Studies* 49, no. 3 (July 2010): 655–80. https://doi.org/10.1086/652014.

Turok, I. "Public Investment and Privatisation in the New Towns: A Financial Assessment of Bracknell." *Environment and Planning A: Economy and Space* 22, no. 10 (1 October 1990): 1323–36. https://doi.org/10.1068/a221323.

UN Human Rights, Office of the High Commissioner. "Guidelines for the Implementation of the Right to Adequate Housing." Accessed 25 April 2022. https://www.ohchr.org/en/special-procedures/sr-housing/guidelines-implementation-right-adequate-housing.

———. "The Impact of Housing Finance Policies on the Right to Adequate Housing of Those Living in Poverty." Accessed 25 April 2022. https://undocs.org/A/67/286.

Wainwright, T. "Looking to Tomorrow: The Past and Future Roles of Securitisation in Residential Mortgage Funding," 2010. https://www.nottingham.ac.uk/business/who-we-are/centres-and-institutes/gcbfi/documents/researchreports/paper80.pdf.

Watson, Matthew. "House Price Keynesianism and the Contradictions of the Modern Investor Subject." *Housing Studies* 25, no. 3 (1 May 2010): 413–26. https://doi.org /10.1080/02673031003711550.

Wheatley, John. *Eight Pound Cottages for Glasgow Citizens.* Glasgow Labour Party, 1913.

Williamson, Philip. *Stanley Baldwin: Conservative Leadership and National Values.* Cambridge University Press, 2007.

Wood, Ellen Meiksins. *Empire of Capital.* Verso, 2005.

———. *The Origin of Capitalism: A Longer View.* Verso, 2002.

Wood, Ian S. *John Wheatley.* Manchester University Press, 1990.

Wordie, J. R. "The Chronology of English Enclosure, 1500–1914." *Economic History Review* 36, no. 4 (1983): 483–505. https://doi.org/10.2307/2597236.

Yelling, James Alfred. "The Incidence of Slum Clearance in England and Wales, 1955–85." *Urban History* 27, no. 2 (2000): 234–54.

———. *Slums and Redevelopment: Policy and Practice in England, 1918–1945, with Particular Reference to London.* UCL Press, 1992.

Index

About the Author

Rebecca Searle is a contemporary historian whose work focuses on the ways in which the study of the past can be used to make critical interventions in the politics of the present. She is a Principal Lecturer at the University of Brighton and Deputy Director of the Centre for Applied Philosophy, Politics and Ethics. Rebecca established and leads the University of Brighton Housing Forum, which brings together researchers, community organisations and policymakers to develop local solutions to the housing crisis in Brighton and Hove.

www.ingramcontent.com/pod-product-compliance
Lightning Source LLC
Chambersburg PA
CBHW022325280326
41932CB00010B/1230